THE DAY
THE WORLD CAME
TO TOWN

THE DAY
THE WORLD CAME
TO TOWN

9/11 in Gander,

Newfoundland

JIM DEFEDE

ReganBooks
An Imprint of HarperCollins*Publishers*

HarperCollins books may be purchased for
educational, business, or sales promotional use.
For information please write: Special Markets
Department, HarperCollins Publishers Inc.,
10 East 53rd Street, New York, NY 10022.

FIRST EDITION

Designed by Judith Stagnitto Abbate

Printed on acid-free paper

Library of Congress Cataloging-in-Publication
Data has been applied for.

ISBN 0-06-051360-8

02 03 04 05 06 RRD 10 9 8 7 6 5 4 3 2 1

For my mother, and in memory of my father

CONTENTS

ACKNOWLEDGMENTS

This book was the idea of Judith Regan, who saw the wonder of this story long before anyone else. I am grateful that she offered me, a relatively unknown writer embarking upon his first book, the opportunity to tackle this project. I'm also indebted to everyone else at ReganBooks and HarperCollins for their assistance, especially Conor Risch, whom I made sweat through several deadlines and whose suggestions made this a better read.

Ultimately, though, the people most responsible for this book are the passengers and townspeople who so generously allowed me into their lives and trusted me to tell their story faithfully. In the course of researching this book, I contacted approximately 180 people, and only one declined to be interviewed. It would be impossible for me to list everyone, so I won't even try. Many brought me into their homes, fed me, and in one case, even tried to take me ice fishing. There are a few, however, whose aid I would like to recognize: Betsy Saunders, from the town government in Gander, who helped me get my bearings when I first arrived in town. Karen Mills and her staff at the Comfort Inn, who not only put up with me for more than a month, but became my de facto secreterial pool. And Professor Pat Byrne, of Memorial University in St. John's, for the afternoon we spent talking about Newfoundland's past, including the history of the so-called Screeching-In ceremony. The description of this in chapter 17 was drawn from these conversations as well as from an article the professor wrote called "Booze, Ritual, and the Invention of Tradition: The Phenomenon of the Newfoundland Screech-In."

Finally, I need to acknowledge the help of my friends and family, particularly Anne Windishar and Jess Walter, whose friendship and support I will always treasure; my sister, Daria, and her husband, Tommy, who are my biggest boosters; my nephews, Conor and Chris, who give me joy; and my mother, Joanne, who makes me want to do my best.

INTRODUCTION

Where are you going?"

The man sitting next to me was curious, since we'd both been on the same plane from Miami to Montreal, and now, by coincidence, we were sitting next to each other on a connecting flight to Halifax, Nova Scotia. It was early February and he was on his way home after vacationing in the Caribbean.

"Gander, Newfoundland," I said.

Because of the lack of a regional accent in my voice, the man could tell Newfoundland was not my home. "Why would anybody leave Miami to go to Gander in the middle of winter?"

This was certainly a reasonable question. When I had left Miami it was warm and sunny and about eighty-five degrees. The forecast in Gander called for temperatures somewhere around minus ten degrees Fahrenheit, with a windchill of minus thirty.

"Don't get me wrong, amazing people in Newfoundland," he quickly added. "I used to live there. Friendliest people you will ever meet. Strangest, too."

The man was a civil engineer and he offered a story as

proof. "We had a crew that was working in this remote town in the far northern end of the province," he began. "The only way to reach this town was by airplane. There were no roads into it at all. And no hotels. So while the crew is working up there, they live with families in the area. The couple they were staying with was really nice, and at the end of the job the company, as a bonus, offered to fly them to Florida for an all-expenses-paid week-long vacation."

The man laughed, recalling what happened next. "The couple turns it down," he explained. "They say, 'But we don't know anyone in Florida, why would we want to go there?' So we ask them if there is someplace they would rather go instead. And they name this town that was about twenty minutes away by plane. They had friends there they hadn't seen in a while. And that's what we did. We flew them to this nearby town, and the couple spent a week with their friends, and then we flew them home again. They said it was the best vacation they had ever been on. That's the kind of folks Newfies are."

He then added: "And you know what happened there on September eleventh?"

∎

There are a few things everyone should know about Newfoundland.

First and foremost is how to pronounce it correctly. Few things are likely to make a native of this province surly faster than mispronouncing their homeland—a fact I was reminded of several times.

Newfoundland is not enunciated as if it were three distinct words, as in "New Found Land." Nor is it pronounced as if it were somehow a Scandinavian colony, as in "New Finland." Instead it is "Newfin-land." The key is to say it very fast. One fellow offered me a simple mnemonic device: "Understand Newfoundland." The words rhyme and the cadence is similar.

Over the centuries, Newfoundlanders have developed a style and language distinctively their own, an amalgam of working-class English and Irish, although in lilt and tone it leans a bit more toward the Irish. The people who originally settled here were not wealthy or well educated. They came for the fish. They were from towns along the southern coast of England—Plymouth and Bristol and Poole—and the west coast of Ireland, places like Ballybunion and Waterville and Galway.

Once they decided to stay in Newfoundland, they created their own style of speech that lives to this day, especially in the smaller outpost towns along the coast. It is more Shakespearean than contemporary. Sentences often end with the phrase "me dear" and "me lovely."

Newfoundlanders employ an almost continuous third-person present tense in their speech. A phrase such as "I am a fisherman" would be "I is a fisherman," or since Newfoundlanders contract "I is" into the single word "I'se" (which sounds like "eyes"), the phrase becomes "I'se be a fisherman." The contractions are often a product of the speed with which they speak. The smaller the town, the faster the talk. There is even something called the *Dictionary of Newfoundland English*, a massive and definitive tome, which is now in its second edition and runs 847 pages.

It is also helpful to remember that Newfoundland is in a world of its own. Or at least its own time zone. Newfoundland is precisely one hour and thirty minutes ahead of U.S. Eastern Standard Time. So when it is 10 A.M. in New York, it is 11:30 A.M. in Gander. When it is noon in Los Angeles, it's 4:30 P.M. in the provincial capital of St. John's. No one else in the world is on Newfoundland time other than Newfies. Which, in a way, is appropriate.

Newfoundlanders are fiercely proud of their history and

remain independent in their identity as Newfoundlanders first and Canadians second. A part of the British Empire since John Cabot landed there in 1497, Newfoundland only became a part of Canada in 1949. The margin of the popular vote in the referendum to join Canada as its last province was so slim that older Newfoundlanders still question the legitimacy of the election. Even today, many Newfoundlanders believe the central government in Ottawa has robbed them of their natural resources and cheated them out of financial well-being.

Newfoundland has an unemployment rate of more than 16 percent, the highest in Canada. Its timber industry is mostly gone, its mines are quickly becoming empty, and the fishing industry—once the lifeblood of Newfoundland—has been decimated, they believe, by the policies of the central government, which prevents small local fisheries from operating but signs treaties to allow foreign trawlers, with their massive nets, to literally scrape the bottom of the Grand Banks and carry off the province's bounty.

Newfoundlanders live like a people under siege. Isolated on an island and powerless against the harshness of the weather, they have learned to count on one another for survival. Neighbor to neighbor. It is a mentality that has been fostered over centuries, since the earliest settlers realized the only way to survive in this desolate but beautiful outpost was to work together. Much of their music captures this spirit. One song in particular that Newfoundlanders love is an old tune called "There Are No Price Tags on the Doors of Newfoundland."

> *Raise your glass and drink with me to that island in the sea*
> *Where friendship is a word they understand.*
> *You will never be alone when you're in a Newfie's home,*
> *There's no price tag on the doors in Newfoundland.*

There will always be a chair at the table for you there,
They will share what they have with any man.
You don't have to worry, friend, if your pocketbook is thin,
There's no price tag on the doors in Newfoundland.

Their willingness to help others is arguably the single most important trait that defines them as Newfoundlanders. Today, it is an identity they cling to, in part, because it is something that cannot be taken away from them.

There is a tale Newfoundlanders are fond of repeating. It is the story of the USS *Truxton*, an American destroyer, and its supply ship, the *Pollux*. On February 18, 1942, a violent storm forced the *Truxton* and the *Pollux* to run aground beneath the cliffs of the Burin Penisula. Both ships broke apart and 193 sailors drowned. But another 186 sailors were saved when the men from the towns of Lawn and Lawrence, at great peril to themselves, descended the icy cliffs to pull them to safety.

"Newfoundlanders are a different breed of people," Gander town constable Oz Fudge told me. "A Newfoundlander likes to put his arm around a person and say, 'It's going to be all right. I'm here. It's going to be okay. We're your friend. We're your buddy. We've got you.' That's the way it's always been. That's the way it always will be. And that's the way it was on September eleventh."

▮

The events of September 11 were historic for many reasons. One of them was that the airspace over the United States was shut down, and every plane in the sky was ordered to land immediately at the nearest available airport.

"Get those goddamn planes down," Transportation Secretary Norman Mineta shouted into a phone from a bunker under the White House.

By the time Mineta uttered those now well-publicized words, American Airlines Flight 11 had already crashed into the North Tower of the World Trade Center, United Airlines Flight 175 had slammed into the South Tower, and American Airlines Flight 77 had struck the Pentagon. A short time later, a fourth plane, United Airlines Flight 93, would plow into a field in a rural area southeast of Pittsburgh. The official order to close U.S. airspace had been given by the Federal Aviation Administration at 9:45 A.M. (Eastern Daylight Time).

Mineta's colorful outburst a few minutes later only added emphasis.

Never before in the ninety-eight-year history of American aviation had such a command been given. There were 4,546 civilian aircraft over the United States at the time, from private Cessnas to jumbo jets, and they all scrambled to find a place to land. Closing airspace had its most disorienting effect, though, on approximately four hundred international flights headed toward the United States, the majority of which were coming across the Atlantic from Europe.

While some of these planes were able to turn around, the only option for most was to land in Canada. Although officials in the United States were certainly justified in wanting to protect their own borders, they were effectively passing the potential threat posed by these planes onto their neighbor. Canadian officials had no way of knowing if any of these flights contained terrorists. In fact, Canadian and American law enforcement suspected there were terrorists lying in wait on some of these flights. Despite the risk, Canada didn't hesitate to accept the orphaned planes.

More than 250 aircraft, carrying 43,895 people, were diverted to fifteen Canadian airports from Vancouver in the west to St. John's in the east. American-bound planes were forced to land in Halifax, Toronto, Ottawa, Montreal, Winnipeg, and Calgary. In each of these cities an army of volunteers and social service agencies came together to help the stranded passengers in any way possible—from offering them a place to stay or a change of clothes to cooking them meals and taking them sightseeing.

Countless stories could be written about the kindness shown in any of these cities. The focus of this book, however, and the purpose for my unseasonable trip this past winter, is Gander, located in the central highlands of Newfoundland. Thirty-eight planes landed there on September 11, depositing 6,595 passengers and crew members in a town whose population is barely 10,000.

For the better part of a week, nearly every man, woman, and child in Gander and the surrounding smaller towns— places with names like Gambo and Appleton and Lewisporte and Norris Arm—stopped what they were doing so they could help. They placed their lives on hold for a group of strangers and asked for nothing in return. They affirmed the basic goodness of man at a time when it was easy to doubt such humanity still existed. If the terrorists had hoped their attacks would reveal the weaknesses in western society, the events in Gander proved its strength.

DAY ONE

Tuesday

September 11

CHAPTER ONE

Clark, Roxanne, and Alexandria Loper, Moscow,
September 10, 2001.

Courtesy of Roxanne Loper

Roxanne and Clark Loper were homeward bound.

Nearly three weeks had passed since they left their ranch outside the small Texas town of Alto and embarked on a journey to adopt a two-year-old girl in the former Soviet republic of Kazakhstan. It was a journey more than fifteen months in the planning and saw the young couple race through airports, bounce along bumpy roads, and wind their way across the Ural Mountains. They dealt with bureaucrats in three different countries and spent their life savings, all for the sake of a child whose picture Roxanne had seen one day on the Internet. Every minute, every dollar, was worth it, though, because now they had Alexandria, and by dinnertime they'd be home.

Over the last seventy-two hours, the three of them had flown from Kazakhstan to Moscow to Frankfurt and were now on the final leg of their trip, a direct flight from Frankfurt to Dallas. They all felt as if they hadn't slept in days. Shortly after takeoff, Alexandria climbed out of her seat and curled up on the floor to take a nap. Roxanne thought about picking her up and strapping her back into her seat, but she knew Alexandria liked sleeping on the floor. She felt comfortable there. It was something the child had grown accustomed to in the orphanage.

As the Lopers' plane, Lufthansa Flight 438, proceeded northwest out of Frankfurt and climbed to above 30,000 feet, Lufthansa Flight 400 began preboarding its first-class passengers. Settling into her seat, Frankfurt mayor Petra Roth was excited about her trip to New York. That night there would be a party in honor of New York City mayor Rudolph Giuliani. Roth and Giuliani had become friends during official visits to each other's city, and Roth was happy to travel the 4,000 miles to pay her respects to the outgoing mayor.

Sitting near Roth was Werner Baldessarini, the chairman of Hugo Boss, who was flying to New York from the company's corporate headquarters in Germany for Fashion Week—an eight-day spectacle of clothes and models in which more than one hundred of the world's top designers show their latest wares in giant tents and on improvised runways. A good show at Fashion Week can guarantee the success of a manufacturer's collection. On Thursday evening, Baldessarini would premier Hugo Boss's Spring 2002 line at Bryant Park in midtown Manhattan. In addition to the financial implications of having a good show, this event was also important to Baldessarini for personal reasons. After twenty-seven years with Hugo Boss, he had made up his mind to retire in 2002. The news hadn't been leaked publicly, but this would be one of his last shows and he wanted it to be a success.

While a flight attendant offered Roth and Baldessarini a glass of champagne before takeoff in Frankfurt, a few hundred miles away in Dublin, George Vitale was taking his seat in coach aboard Continental Flight 23. As one of the people responsible for protecting New York governor George Pataki on a day-to-day basis, Vitale had flown to Ireland in early September to make advance security arrangements for the governor's visit there later that month. Unfortunately, a fresh round of violence in Northern Ireland caused the governor to abruptly cancel his trip, and the New York State trooper was told to come home.

If he had wanted to, Vitale could have stayed in Ireland to see friends and family. The forty-three-year-old is half Irish and he's made several trips over the years to the Emerald Isle. This wasn't a good time for a vacation, however. He had a number of responsibilities waiting for him at home in Brooklyn. In addition to being a senior investigator with the state police, Vitale was also taking night classes toward a degree in education. Assuming everything went smoothly, he'd be home in time for his class at Brooklyn College.

An hour after Vitale's flight ascended into the sky, Hannah O'Rourke stood outside the boarding area for Aer Lingus Flight 105 and cried as she hugged brothers and sisters good-bye. The sixty-six-year-old O'Rourke was born in Ireland's County Monaghan, about forty miles north of Dublin, but had emigrated to the United States nearly fifty years ago. She made a good life for herself in America. Along with her husband, Dennis, she raised three children and now lived on Long Island.

In recent years, she'd returned to Ireland as often as possible to see her family. This time around, she spent three weeks in the countryside with her husband. She hated saying good-bye to her kin, but her family in America was eager for her to come home. Waiting to board the plane, O'Rourke dreaded the flight back. It was no secret she hated flying, especially over water.

The scene was no less emotional for fellow passenger Maria O'Driscoll. Although the two women didn't know each other, the seventy-year-old O'Driscoll was born in County Louth, a stone's throw from O'Rourke's birthplace. O'Driscoll had come to the United States when she was a young woman. Her reason was simple: "I fell in love with a Yank." That was back in 1954.

Standing alongside her at the airport in Dublin was her husband, Lenny.

Lenny O'Driscoll wasn't "the Yank" that prompted Maria to move to America. That fellow, Maria's first husband, died in 1987. When Lenny met Maria a short time later, he, too, had lost a spouse. They married in 1993, and since then, they had been over to Ireland almost every year.

The occasion for this trip—not that they ever needed one— was the wedding of Maria's niece. Of her six brothers and sisters, Maria had been the only one to come to America. They all stayed in the Irish Sea town of Dundalk.

Lenny's ancestors were Irish, but he was born in Newfoundland, so the good-byes every year at the end of their trip weren't as painful to him as they were to Maria. He knew she would be sad and quiet on the flight home. There must be a way to cheer her up, he thought. He decided he'd think it over as soon as the plane took off.

How *aboot* this weather?"

"Beautiful."

"Delightful."

"Cold's gonna come soon, buddy."

"And the snow."

"Ay, she's gotta come sometime."

Inside the local coffee shop, the unseasonably warm weather was all anyone could talk about, including Gander mayor Claude Elliott. Since becoming mayor in 1996, Elliott liked to start each morning at Tim Horton's, the Canadian equivalent of Starbucks. Elliott rode to political power on the strength of a snowmobile—or, as they are more commonly referred to in Gander, a Ski-doo. In 1989, members of the town council wanted to ban Ski-doos from operating inside the city limits. Elliott helped lead an uprising against the ban, and in 1990 he was elected to the town council.

Like any small-town mayor, Elliott knew how important it was to keep in touch with what folks were talking about. On this day it was the weather. This was the warmest September anyone could recall in a decade. Temperatures were around twenty-one degrees Celsius, about seventy degrees Fahrenheit.

The local economy was another coffee-klatch topic. The unemployment rate in Gander wasn't as high as on the rest of the island, but people were still looking for new ways to stimulate business. They'd certainly had their boondoggles. A few years before, they attempted to turn Gander into ski resort, a project that had ultimately failed.

After an hour or so at the coffeehouse, the mayor headed over to town hall.

Meanwhile, Oz Fudge was making the morning rounds in his patrol car. One of only two town constables in Gander, Fudge used to be with the Royal Canadian Mounted Police. That was more than twenty years ago. For the last fifteen years, the forty-seven-year-old has worked exclusively for the town.

In Gander, the RCMP handles investigations into serious

crimes, and Fudge handles more community-oriented problems. He makes traffic stops and helps round up stray animals.
If a husband and wife are arguing a little too loud for the
neighbors, Fudge calms them down. If a couple of knuckle-
heads start throwing punches in a bar, Fudge is the one to
break them up.

He doesn't carry a gun, doesn't like them, and as far as
he's concerned, he doesn't need one. Guns only make people
nervous. A few years ago, the RCMP provided him with a bul-
letproof vest. There had been some drug smuggling in the
area, and since Fudge was making traffic stops, the Mounties
were concerned he might inadvertently pull over a gun-toting
smuggler on his way through town. Fudge wore it for two
weeks, but took it off because it was so darn uncomfortable. He
hasn't worn it since.

Fudge was born in Lewisporte—about forty minutes from
Gander—where his father used to work out at the military base.
Fudge and his wife, whom he refers to as "the War Department," have three kids. He named his oldest son after his
favorite actor, Jimmy Stewart, who starred in his favorite
movie, *It's a Wonderful Life*. He coaches his daughter's basket-
ball team. The team's not very good, but then again, he's not
much of a coach. It's all for fun anyway.

A school bus drivers' strike in the district meant most kids
were either walking to school that morning or being dropped
off by their parents, so Fudge was paying close attention to the
crosswalks and streets nearest the schools to make sure no one
was speeding. Once the kids were tucked away in school, he
continued on with his normal patrol.

The streets in Gander are laid out in an unusual fashion.
Rather than laying out a simple grid, the town's forefathers
thought it would be unique to twist and turn the main perimeter roads into the profile of a male goose's head. Memorial
Drive forms the base of the neck; Elizabeth Drive curves up to

form the back and top of the head and then swoops back down to meet with Edinburgh Street to create the bird's beak. When most people look at a map of the town, the gander image doesn't strike them right away, but as soon as someone points it out, it's impossible to miss. Trees line most of the streets in Gander, while the majority of homes are modest, two-story structures with small, neatly trimmed lawns and backyards. And although the town is relatively flat, it sits perched above Lake Gander, a long thin body of water that feeds into the Gander River and ultimately the Atlantic Ocean. Fudge liked the quiet nature of his town. And on this morning, he'd seen nothing out of the ordinary.

By midmorning Fudge was sitting in his patrol car in the parking lot of the curling club, wondering how he was going to keep himself busy for the rest of the day, when Bonnie Harris ran up. "Turn on the radio," she yelled. "You're not going to believe what's going on."

Fudge flipped over to the CBC radio news channel.

"Holy God," he cried, and then sped off for town hall.

▌

Halfway between Frankfurt and New York City, Captain Reinhard Knoth switched his plane's radio to Unicom, a frequency shared by all pilots. Unicom allows planes from different airlines to pass information to one another about weather conditions or delays at airports. A pilot for Lufthansa for thirty years, Knoth had made this transatlantic run more times than he could remember. He was flying an older-model 747, his altitude was 30,000 feet, and he was cruising along at just under six hundred miles per hour. The sky was blue, the air calm, the horizon clear. Turning on the autopilot, Knoth was listening to the casual banter between planes when a pilot for

KLM broke in excitedly. "There's something happening in New York," the captain declared. "An accident."

Knoth turned his radio to the commercial frequency for the BBC. The station was broadcasting live from New York, and the announcer reported an explosion at the World Trade Center, possibly caused by an airplane crashing into the North Tower. Knoth was dumbfounded. He looked over at his copilot and his flight engineer to make sure they heard this as well.

How could a plane crash into one of the towers? It didn't seem possible. His copilot speculated it must have been a small, private plane. Maybe the pilot had a heart attack or blacked out. Even so, what were the odds of a plane accidentally hitting a skyscraper? There was that time back in 1945, they recalled, when an army pilot, lost in fog, crashed his B-25 into the Empire State Building. But that was so long ago, and approach patterns and the rules for flying over Manhattan were different now. As they talked, the BBC broadcast caught their attention once again.

"... another explosion ... a second plane has hit the World Trade Center!"

A second plane? Two planes had hit the towers? Clearly, this wasn't an accident. It was 9:03 A.M. in New York, and Knoth bounced from one radio frequency to another, scavenging bits of information. One fact was certain: even with a gun to his head, no airline pilot would deliberately crash his plane into the Trade Center. Knoth knew someone other than the pilot must have been flying those planes.

Knoth wasn't the only person to realize this. On Unicom, pilots were alerting one another to be careful. Every plane in the air could be a possible target for hijackers. With each passing minute, the voices of pilots broadcasting over Unicom grew more frantic. Did anyone know which airlines were involved? Was it American? United? Delta? Did anyone hear a flight number? How many other planes were unaccounted for? One? Two? Five? Nine?

By 9:15, Knoth was informed that all airports in the New York City area had been shut down. Unsure of what to do, he sent an urgent message to Lufthansa's base in Frankfurt asking for guidance. He was still almost four hours from New York. Should he continue on to the United States and possibly land elsewhere, or turn around and fly back to Germany? Turning a plane around is no easy maneuver. When one plane turns around, it has a ripple effect on every plane in the air, and so it needs to be carefully choreographed.

A decision needed to be made quickly. Knoth was approaching the halfway point in the Atlantic, thirty degrees longitude; the invisible line of no return for airline pilots. Once pilots cross that mark, they are usually committed to flying to their destination. As he waited for instructions, Knoth wondered about the 354 passengers aboard his plane, Lufthansa Flight 400. Were any of them a threat? If there were terrorists on board, they might have been waiting until the plane was closer to the United States before trying something. Knoth glanced behind him to the cockpit door. It wasn't very sturdy. And then he realized something else: it wasn't even locked.

CHAPTER TWO

Bonnie Harris, Constable Oz Fudge, and Linda Humby.

Harold O'Reilly didn't want to think about his birthday. And he certainly didn't want any fuss just because he was turning fifty. He'd work his regular shift at Gander's air-traffic control center and then celebrate that night by going out to dinner with his wife and family. Located less than a mile from Gander International Airport, the center, commonly referred to as ATC, is a bunkerlike building that keeps track of all flights between Europe and North America. Every day nearly a thousand flights cross the Atlantic. To keep these planes from bumping into one another, there are approximately forty controllers on duty, each responsible for a different patch of the sky over the water. If plane is headed toward the United States, once it passes Newfoundland, the controller hands the flight over to his or her counterpart in Montreal or Boston or New York. If a plane is going to Europe, then once it reaches the other side of the ocean, the flight is given to centers in Ireland or France or Spain.

Generally speaking, being a controller in Gander is not as high-pressured as being a controller in a major metropolitan area, where you have hundreds of flights bunched together in a very small space of sky. In those centers the overriding concern is to prevent a midair collision.

Gander controllers worry about this as well, but planes flying across the Atlantic are spaced far enough apart to make it less of a threat. Instead, with long oceanic flights it's all about the jet stream, that ribbon of air that can save a pilot fuel and help him reach his destination a little sooner. Finding the precise altitude of the stream on any given day and easing pilots into it is the art of being a controller in Gander. Gander controllers take pride in making sure pilots and their passengers get from one point on the map to another as smoothly and as comfortably as possible.

Fittingly, the inside of the building where they oversee the journeys of so many travelers has an eerily intense feel to it. There are no windows and the lights in the main rooms are kept low in order to prevent glare on the screens from disrupting the vision of the controllers. As a result, the controllers appear supernatural, bathed in the artificial glow of their own monitors as they control the skies over the Atlantic.

O'Reilly has been coming to work at the Gander ATC for twenty-eight years. He grew up in a small town of a few hundred people in a corner of Newfoundland accessible only by ferry. He was a high-school teacher for a short time, but wanted to try something different. Being an air-traffic controller certainly fit that description. And now he was the boss.

As the lead supervisor, he was the man in charge of operations. It was his center, his air. He'd been at work a couple of hours when someone told him to come see the television in the break room because a plane had just slammed into the World Trade Center. He arrived just as the second plane hit. His horror was quickly replaced by a feeling of dread that there was more to come. Obviously the airports in New York were going to be closed, O'Reilly concluded. But even he was surprised when he received a call from the air-traffic control center in Boston alerting him that all airspace in the United States had been closed.

The second piece of news from Boston: all American carriers—United, American, Delta, Continental—had to land at the nearest airport immediately. Foreign carriers had a choice: they could turn around and fly home or land in Canada, but they couldn't come into the United States. As O'Reilly talked to Federal Aviation Administration officials in Boston, American Airlines Flight 77 crashed into the Pentagon.

September 11 was certainly shaping up to be an unbelievable birthday.

O'Reilly called his supervisors together. He'd worked with most of these men for years and trusted their judgment. By now everyone in the building knew about the disaster in New York, and as he briefed his supervisors, he tried to read their faces to see if any betrayed a sense of fear or apprehension. If they were scared, O'Reilly thought to himself, they certainly weren't showing it. Instead everyone seemed anxious to confront the challenge ahead.

There were about three hundred planes in their airspace and all of them had to be rerouted and given alternate landing sites. The planes were going to have to change altitudes, change directions, and converge on a few airports in eastern Canada. Pilots were already hailing the center, trying to figure out what they were supposed to do. O'Reilly kept it simple with just one instruction for his supervisors: "Let's just get those planes on the ground, as soon as possible, without having any accidents."

His supervisors might not have been afraid, but O'Reilly was privately terrified that there would be an accident. It wasn't a question of his not having confidence in the ability of his controllers. The problem in his mind was that there were just too many planes and, because they all had to land as quickly as possible, too little time to see them all in safely.

Without being called, off-duty controllers started arriving at the center within a half hour of the attacks. Eventually every controller working a screen had at least one backup and a supervisor to help. There was no real plan or thought given to which planes should land where. The controllers started dividing planes up among a handful of airports that could accommodate them. St. John's and Stephenville in Newfound-land, Moncton in New Brunswick, Halifax in Nova Scotia, as well as the airports in larger cities like Montreal, Quebec, and even Toronto.

The key for O'Reilly, however, was Gander.

∎

Built in the mid-thirties, the airport in Gander was initially a military base shared by the United States, England, and Canada. When it opened in 1938, it was the largest airport in the world. Its runways were designed to accommodate the heaviest planes of the day, and the base played a critical role during World War II. Supplies and troops on their way to

Europe from the United States needed to land in Gander to refuel for the transatlantic journey. More than 20,000 fighters and heavy bombers manufactured in the United States stopped in Gander before joining the war in Europe.

After the war, the landing field focused its attention on commercial flights. Through the late forties and fifties, most overseas commercial flights out of the United States and Canada refueled in Gander. Gander International Airport became known as the biggest gas station in the world, and as air traffic grew, so did a community. The town of Gander didn't even exist prior to the creation of the airport and its hopes were built on the promise of aviation. Many of its streets are named for famous aviators, names like Yeager, Byrd, and Lindbergh. Even its businesses adopted an aviation theme. Gander's most famous bar was the Flyer's Club, a notoriously raucous pub in the center of town.

At the height of the Cold War in the sixties and seventies, Gander had another distinction. It was the spot where hundreds of people every year defected from Eastern Europe and Cuba. All of the airline traffic between Fidel Castro's Cuba and the Soviet Union and its satellites stopped in Gander to refuel. When an Aeroflot flight between Havana and Moscow or East Berlin touched down in Gander and the passengers were allowed off the plane while it was being serviced, some of the passengers invariably would ask Canadian officials for asylum. For a time Gander was dubbed "defection heaven."

So many East Germans defected in Gander that West Germany actually set up special consulate offices there to help the asylum seekers reach their ultimate goal of getting to the democratic side of their divided nation. For many, the quickest path from East Berlin to West Berlin didn't involve jumping the wall, but flying through Gander. Of course, not everyone defected. Castro stopped in Gander on so many occasions that locals have lost track of the precise number.

During one lengthy layover, a local resident even took the Cuban dictator on a toboggan ride through town.

The advent of the jet engine in the sixties, however, was the beginning of the end of Gander's prosperity. And the introduction of the Boeing 747 in 1970, with its increased fuel capacity and longer flying times, was a technological breakthrough that guaranteed Gander's demise as a commercial airline hub. As more and more airlines replaced their aging fleets with these newer aircraft, the town named after a male goose started feeling the heat. Property prices fell as many airlines pulled out of Gander completely.

The eighties and nineties found Gander's airport used primarily as a refueling stop by a few charter outfits and the American military. On December 12, 1985, an Arrow Air charter flight crashed a half mile from the airport shortly after takeoff, killing everyone on board, including 248 members of the U.S. Army's 101st Airborne Division. They were on their way home to North Carolina for Christmas following a peacekeeping mission in the Sinai Peninsula. The Arrow crash remains the worst airplane disaster in Canada's history.

For the past three decades Gander has remained a frequent stopover point for private and corporate jets. Celebrities and CEOs of major corporations have visited the airport's DVL—Distinguished Visitors' Lounge—before continuing on their trip to Cannes or London or Rome. Airport employees have grown used to seeing folks like Frank Sinatra, John Wayne, Lee Iacocca, John Travolta, Oprah Winfrey, Brad Pitt, Nicole Kidman, or Tom Cruise. In the last twenty years, at least twenty-five heads of state have passed through Gander.

At the start of the new millennium, Gander's civic pride in aviation matters rested on the airport's designation a few years before as an alternate site for the Space Shuttle to land if it has to abort its mission shortly after takeoff. And now, on September 11, for the same reason it was considered a suitable landing site for the Space Shuttle—it has an unusually long main run-way—Harold O'Reilly knew it would be the ideal place to handle a sky full of jumbo jets with nowhere to land.

The irony of the situation was not lost on O'Reilly. The very same planes that had rendered Gander's airport largely obsolete were now going to be forced to seek shelter there.

∎

The television set in Gander's town hall didn't have cable. The local stations had interrupted their regular programming for bulletins out of New York, but the reception wasn't very good. Nevertheless, town employees gathered around and gazed in horror. Mayor Elliott watched for a few minutes and then decided to go home, where he could follow the coverage on CNN.

Inside his house, he stared at his television in absolute disbelief. As the towers became engulfed in flames, he kept glancing at the word LIVE in the corner of the screen. This wasn't some movie, he thought to himself, this was actually happening right now. Before long, Elliott received a phone call from the town manager. Officials at the airport had called. U.S. airspace was closed and a lot of planes were being diverted to Canada. It looked like Gander was going to be receiving a sizable portion of them, perhaps as many as fifty planes.

"What about the passengers?" Elliott asked.

For now, he was told, the plan was to allow the jets to land, but to hold all of the passengers on board until U.S. airspace opened up again and the planes could take off. They would probably be on the ground for only a few hours.

Elliott knew better. Watching events unfold on his television, he could see that the United States was in a state of chaos. The whereabouts of the president were unclear. The American military was mobilizing. Nobody seemed to have an understanding of what was happening. This was obviously going to take time to sort out, certainly more than a few hours. The mayor then started doing the math. If there were fifty planes en route, with an average of 250 passengers and crew members on each plane, they could easily have more than 12,000 people landing in Gander in the next few hours. Even if they never got off the plane, just having to feed that many people would be a tremendous undertaking for a town the size of Gander.

Elliott didn't want to get caught flat-footed. The town needed to start getting ready in case the passengers were going to be stranded there overnight. The town opened its emergency operations center—a room inside town hall—and started contacting local groups to place them on alert that it might need their assistance.

❙

Geoff Tucker was already making preparations at the airport. He'd worked at Gander International for nineteen years and was now the vice-president of the local airport authority. With the airport director out of town for a conference, Tucker was the man in charge.

He was alerted to the attacks in New York by Bruce Terris, the supervisor up in the airport's tower. Right away Tucker knew the ripple from such a catastrophe would find its way to Gander. "The lifeboat of the North Atlantic" is the way he always referred to Gander International. Every pilot who flies to the United States from Europe knows exactly where Gander is located. If there is a serious mechanical problem over the ocean or a passenger has a heart attack or goes berserk with a case of air rage, the pilot makes an emergency landing in Gander.

After receiving the call from the tower, Tucker met with the head of the local detachment of the Royal Canadian Mounted Police, the commander of the Canadian military base in Gander, as well as local and federal government officials. They all knew an onslaught was about to hit them. The RCMP and the central government in Ottawa were adamant, though: the planes could land, but nobody would be allowed off.

▌

O'Reilly was amazed at how calmly his controllers were handling the situation. Their first task was to contact all of the planes currently heading for the United States. During that first hour not all of the pilots had heard about the attack, and controllers were told to tell pilots only that "a crisis" in the United States had forced the government to close down its airspace. The pilots had the choice of turning around and returning to Europe or landing in Canada.

Even if pilots asked questions about the events in New York, the controllers were told not to discuss the attack with them. They weren't there to provide news updates or answer questions or knock down rumors, their only concern was to get the planes safely on the ground. The truth was that the controllers weren't the best source for information anyway. The pilots had access to commercial radio stations, while the controllers were working the screens.

Dwayne Puddister, a controller for ten years, was working "high altitude," meaning planes above 28,000 feet. By the time they came into his territory, most planes were already committed to landing in Canada, so Puddister didn't offer them a lot of options.

"There is a crisis in the United States and airspace is

closed," he'd say. "You can land in either St. John's or Gander. You have thirty seconds to decide. After that, I'll decide for you."

Less than a minute later Puddister would come back to them.

"Have you made up your mind?"

If the pilot tried to stall, Puddister would make the decision.

"You're *instructed* to land . . ." And then he'd fill in the blank. The word "instruct" carries a lot of weight in the vernacular of pilots and air-traffic controllers. As a matter of civility, pilots and controllers normally use the word "request." When a controller uses the word "instruct," it's the same as an order. A pilots who refuses to comply can lose his license.

One pilot of a private jet, after being given a choice between Gander and St. John's, started arguing with Puddister, telling the controller he wanted to press ahead to his original destination in the United States. The pilot was flying a Gulfstream V, one of the most expensive and luxurious corporate jets ever made. It was clear to Puddister that the pilot wasn't aware of the attacks in New York and Washington.

"You will not be going to the United States today," Puddister said. "You are *instructed* to land in St. John's."

"You have no idea," the pilot argued. "We have well-to-do people on board."

"*You* have no idea," Puddister shot back. "I don't care who you have on board. You're going to be landing in St. John's. Now I have no time to deal with your foolishness."

Fellow controller Reg Batson was even more blunt with the pilots.

"Anyone trying to enter U.S. airspace," he warned, "will be shot down."

Batson was juggling ten times the number of aircraft on

his screen that he'd have under normal conditions. As a result, he urged the pilots to stay alert. Broadcasting on a channel for all of the pilots entering his airspace, Batson confided his concern and made an unusually frank request.

"There's a lot happening," he told the pilots, "and it's going to be hard to keep track of all of you. Pay attention to your proximity alarms," he continued, "and keep looking out your windows for other aircraft."

Pilots were on their own as to what they would tell their passengers. They could lie and announce they were landing in Canada because of minor mechanical problems; they could say one of the passengers was ill and they needed to land at the nearest airport for medical reasons; or they could tell the truth.

Whatever they told their passengers, nearly all of the pilots decided to wait until just before they were ready to land to announce that they would be landing in Canada. No sense provoking a possible terrorist on board into action, they all reasoned.

▮

Thirty minutes after asking for guidance from Lufthansa's base in Frankfurt, Captain Knoth still hadn't heard back from anyone. While he continued to wait, Knoth summoned the plane's chief purser into the cockpit to brief him about the attacks in New York and Washington. He told the purser not to discuss what was happening with any of the other flight attendants, and to certainly keep the news from the passengers. They were still almost two hours from Canada and Knoth didn't want to spark a panic, or worse, provoke any terrorists who might have been on board. He ordered the purser to barricade the spiral staircase leading to the cockpit and the first-class section of the plane. He told him to use the food-and-beverage carts to block the access to the stairwell and lock them in place. It wouldn't stop a determined hijacker for long, Knoth thought, but it would slow him down and give the crew a chance to react.

By the time Lufthansa Flight 400 reached the halfway point across the Atlantic, Knoth still hadn't heard from Frankfurt. He made the decision on his own: he was going to continue west rather than turn around. Knoth contacted Gander's air-traffic control center for clearance to fly on to Toronto's airport. Lufthansa had a large base of operations in Toronto, and Knoth assumed they'd best be able to serve the passengers who would likely be stranded for several days.

"Request denied," the controller in Gander said bluntly. "You have to land now."

The controller gave him his options—all in Newfoundland. Through a bizarre coincidence, Knoth happened to have spent time in a flight simulator several months earlier making emergency landings. One of the airports he practiced for was Gander International. And like most transatlantic pilots, Knoth carried maps in his flight bag showing the layout of the airport and its runways.

"We'll take Gander," he said.

▌

A little before 11 A.M. local time, Virgin Air Flight 75, on its way from Manchester, England, to Orlando, Florida, became the first diverted airplane to land in Gander. The plane circled the town, came in low from the northeast, and landed on Runway 22. Aboard were 337 passengers, most on their way to a family vacation in Disney World.

The plane taxied to the terminal and stopped. A small contingent of police took up points around the plane as passengers stared out the windows. A movable staircase, used to remove passengers from the plane, remained untouched, just out of sight of the aircraft.

CHAPTER THREE

Brooklyn's Rescue 2 (Kevin O'Rourke is the second from the right).

Roxanne Loper lurched forward as the pilot of Lufthansa Flight 438 cut his speed and made a hard right turn. As the plane dramatically slowed, she grabbed her husband's hand to steady herself and then reached for two-year-old Alexandria, still asleep on the floor of the plane. She scooped the child into her arms and wondered what was happening. Was it bad weather? An air pocket? Was there something mechanically wrong with the plane?

On the back of the seat in front of her a small television

displayed the aircraft's speed and projected path from Frankfurt to Dallas. Roxanne watched as the numbers indicating the plane's airspeed dropped from 600 mph to almost 300 mph. She could also see that they were no longer on their original course. Rather than heading west, they were now tracking due north, away from the United States. They were still over the Atlantic, but the pilot seemed to be heading for the nearest available point on the map. Roxanne could feel her heart racing. Was the pilot trying to reach land? Was he was afraid of crashing into the water?

Although it felt much longer, within a few seconds the pilot came over the loudspeaker. He spoke in German and Roxanne couldn't discern much from the tone of his voice. Then she heard the passengers who could understand him audibly gasp. This made her even more frightened. Finally, in somewhat broken English, the pilot announced that airspace over the United States was closed and he had been ordered to land in Gander, Newfoundland. He offered no further explanation.

"We'll be on the ground in thirty minutes," he said.

An older gentleman sitting in front of Roxanne turned to her. He seemed confused. In all his years of traveling, he said, he'd never heard of the United States closing its airspace. "Never," the man kept saying. "Never."

Throughout the plane, strangers talked to one another, nervously speculating about what might be occurring. Some asked if there could have been a plane crash in the United States. But that didn't make sense. The government had never shut down the entire aviation system when there was an accident. It must be something worse.

A bomb? But that, too, would affect only one plane.

An attack? Could the United States be under attack? My God, what kind of attack? And from whom? Passengers began imagining the worst. They asked the flight attendants for more information. The attendants swore they knew nothing else. Murmured prayers rolled through the plane.

Roxanne's husband, Clark, was now holding Alexandria. It had been only six days since their adoption of the girl became final. After months of wrangling their way through the bureaucratic maze of adopting a child overseas, Roxanne had thought the worst was behind her. Now she was uncertain about what lay ahead.

So much in her life had already changed—she couldn't help but think back on it all. Had it really been fifteen months since she first saw Alexandria's picture on the Internet?

After trying unsuccessfully to have a child of their own, they decided to adopt one. Roxanne was searching various adoption Web sites when she came across one for World Partners and spotted Alexandria, who was then only nine months old. There was something about this baby that was special to Roxanne, a connection she hadn't felt before.

When the couple contacted World Partners, they discovered Alexandria was no longer available. Undeterred, they continued talking to the counselors at the adoption agency and decided to provide a home for another child, a three-month-old baby they would name Samantha. Like Alexandria, Samantha had been born in Kazakhstan, a country in Central Asia populated by people of Mongolian and Turkish descent.

Most Americans who traveled this far to adopt a child usually went to Russia or Romania so they could find a "white" baby, one that would look like them. Roxanne and Clark were different. They chose Kazakhstan because they didn't care if their adoptive child's skin was a different color from their own. They were just looking for a child to love. And it didn't matter how far they had to go to find one.

To be sure, Kazakhstan is a long way from their home in Alto, Texas, population 1,053. Roxanne, twenty-nine, and

Clark, thirty-three, own an 850-acre ranch outside the East Texas town, located about two hours southeast of Dallas. They have horses, chickens, cows, and a few hundred acres of pine, which they plan on foresting.

In June 2000, the couple made the arduous journey to Kazakhstan to adopt Samantha. They spent nearly a month in the country, and when it was all over and they arrived home with the baby, the adoption had cost them almost $25,000.

And then, early in 2001, Roxanne was scrolling through the Web site for World Partners and once again saw Alexandria's picture. The child was older, but Roxanne had no doubt that it was her. She contacted the agency and learned it was indeed the same child she'd seen a year earlier. She had no idea why Alexandria was suddenly now available, nor did she care. She told Clark it was time Samantha had a sister.

They scraped together the rest of their savings and started the adoption process all over again. On August 18, they flew from Dallas to Frankfurt and then on to Samara, Russia, an industrial center five hundred miles southeast of Moscow. From there they spent six hours traveling by car along bumpy roads across the Ural Mountains into Kazakhstan, a country whose southern border is less than two hundred miles from Afghanistan.

Located in the town of Uralsk, the orphanage was known simply as Baby House Number Two. The orphanage was an industrial-looking building with a forbidding black gate in front, and was surrounded by a barren dirt field where the children would play. Despite the ominous facade, the government facility was clean and the children well cared for. There were about eighty kids in this particular orphanage, ranging in age from newborns to four-year-olds.

They arrived in Uralsk at four in the morning on August 20, and checked into a run-down hotel near the baby house. For the next fourteen days, they would visit the orphanage and

spend two hours in the morning and two hours in the afternoon playing with Alexandria so the child would get to know
them. Alexandria instantly loved Clark but couldn't stand
Roxanne. Whenever they arrived, she would run to Clark and
throw a fit if Roxanne tried to hold her.

On September 5, the couple flew across Kazakhstan to the
city of Almaty for a court hearing to have the adoption final-
ized. The child was turned over to them, and on September 9
they all flew to Moscow. The United States requires couples
adopting children in Kazakhstan to present themselves at the
American embassy in Moscow so the child can receive a phys-
ical from an American doctor and a visa to travel.

They left Russia on September 11 at 3 A.M. for Frankfurt,
arriving in time for their connecting flight to Dallas. They
weren't the only couple on board Lufthansa Flight 438 bringing home a Kazakh orphan.

Beth and Billy Wakefield had also adopted a baby girl
through the World Partners program, an eleven-month-old
by the name of Diana. The two couples had traveled together
from Dallas, split up in Kazakhstan because Diana was in an
orphanage in a different city than Alexandria's, and then reunited in Almaty.

The two families flew together to Moscow and then on to
Germany, and now, they thought, they were all on their way
home. They'd be back in Dallas in a few hours. Once there, the
Wakefields and their new daughter, Diana, were scheduled to
catch a plane to Nashville, where a large contingent of friends
and family would be waiting to greet them at the airport.

Roxanne and Clark would say their good-byes in Dallas,
and after the Wakefields left, they would drive home to Alto
and a big homecoming as well. Roxanne was anxious to get
there. This had been the longest she had ever been away from
Samantha and she missed her terribly.

The plane wasn't full, so the couples were able to stretch

out with the kids and not feel cramped. Alexandria slept on the floor. Diana was a bit fussy and didn't want to sleep. After a grueling three weeks, both the Lopers and the Wakefields were mentally and physically exhausted. The travel, the bureaucracies, the paperwork, the language barriers, the food, the living conditions had all taken their toll. This was an ordeal they'd been more than willing to go through to adopt a child, but they were relieved that the worst was behind them. As far as they could tell, there were no more hurdles to cross, no more worries to overcome. Just a few more hours and they would be home. A few more hours and they could shower in their own homes, sleep in their own beds, eat in their own kitchens. Just a few more hours and they would have their lives back. As that idea sank in, they all began to relax.

And then the plane suddenly banked right. Thirty minutes later they were in Gander.

▌

Except for the pilot and his crew, no one aboard Aer Lingus Flight 105 had any reason to suspect something was wrong. The only thing troubling Lenny O'Driscoll was his wife. They were several hours into their flight home from Ireland, and Lenny was still trying to think of something he could do to cheer Maria up.

Looking over a map, Lenny noticed that the flight path from Dublin to New York would take them past Newfoundland. And that's when it occurred to him.

"You know, Maria, I've never taken you to Newfoundland," he said. "I've got to take you there sometime. We should plan another trip."

Lenny hadn't been to Newfoundland in thirty-five years. He'd been born in Bay Bulls, a fishing community outside St.

John's, but left to find work in the United States. Maria thought a trip to Newfoundland was a glorious idea. Nothing cheered her up like the prospect of a new adventure. Twenty minutes later the pilot came on the public-address system to announce that there was a problem in the United States and they were being ordered to land at the nearest available airport.

"We'll be landing in Gander, Newfoundland," the pilot declared.

Maria and Lenny couldn't believe their ears. "Well, it looks like I'm taking you to Newfoundland now after all." Lenny laughed uncomfortably.

Sitting in the back of the same plane, Hannah and Dennis O'Rourke listened intently as the pilot explained the situation.

"Terrorists have struck the Twin Towers," the pilot declared. "I'll keep you informed as I learn more. Please stay calm."

Hannah's thoughts immediately went to her son Kevin, a New York City firefighter for eighteen years. He was a member of one of the department's elite fire rescue teams. His firehouse was located just across the bridge from Manhattan, in Brooklyn, and if he was on duty, he'd likely be in the center of danger.

"Maybe he wasn't working today," Hannah told Dennis, who nodded softly.

Hannah did the only thing she could. She closed her eyes and prayed.

Also traveling with them was Hannah's nephew Brendan Boylan and his girlfriend, Amanda. Once they landed in Gander, the family huddled together to support one another. They had no idea how long they would be on the ground or when they'd be able to get off the plane.

As passengers began using their cell phones to call home, word began spreading through the plane about the seriousness of the disaster in New York. Upon learning that the parents of a firefighter were on the plane, several of the passengers walked over to them to offer their own prayers for the son's safety.

A man on the flight offered Hannah his cell phone so she could call her family. Hannah reached her daughter, Patricia, in Cedarhurst, Long Island.

Before the attack, Patricia had been out to the supermarket, shopping for a few groceries so her parents wouldn't come home to an empty refrigerator. As she was driving home from the store, she listened in horror to the news bulletins on the radio. Since then, she'd been trying to find out what happened to her parents' flight. Initially, she was told all of the flights from Europe had been turned around and that her mother and father were on their way back to Dublin. Frantically, she contacted her relatives in Ireland to alert them that her parents would be back there that afternoon.

While Patricia was still busy trying to arrange for someone to pick up her parents at the airport in Dublin, her phone rang. It was Hannah.

"Is Kevin working?" Hannah asked, not wasting any time on pleasantries.

"Yeah, Ma, he is," Patricia answered.

"Has anyone heard from him? Is he all right?"

"No one's heard," Patricia said. "But I'm sure he's fine."

Patricia wasn't just saying this to comfort her mother. She believed it. She knew her big brother and he wasn't the type to stop and make a phone call in the middle of a crisis. He'd been in tough circumstances before, and he'd always handled it the same way: he'd get caught up in his job, and when it was over he'd call and tell everyone what an amazing experience it was.

"Where are you?" Patricia finally asked.

"Nova Scotia," Hannah mistakenly said. With all of the commotion, she had apparently misheard the pilot. "I have to go," she continued. "There are other people waiting to use this phone."

"Don't worry, Ma," Patricia repeated. "Kevin will be fine. He'll come home."

█

Hannah knew Patricia was right. Kevin had certainly made it through some close calls in the past. Just a few weeks earlier, he had been summoned to rescue a man who had tried to commit suicide by jumping into the Hudson River. Kevin was one of the first firefighters on the scene. Donning his scuba gear, he knew it was risky to jump from the pier into the dark water because he would have no way of knowing if there were any objects lurking just below the surface. He dove in anyway and crashed into an underwater piling, injuring his leg. Nevertheless, he carried on with the rescue and saved the man's life. A month prior to that, he helped save an elderly woman from an apartment fire in Brooklyn. When the woman's son came to the station house a month later to thank everyone, he offered the firefighters his life savings, $2,000, as a sign of his appreciation. Of course they refused, but it was Kevin's idea to tell the man to take the money and buy smoke detectors for the homes of his loved ones. Hannah was so proud of that.

At times Kevin would get close enough to a blaze that it would melt his equipment. His captain would scold him about the risks he took, but Kevin didn't know how to do the job any other way. During his career with the department he'd received four individual citations for valor and shared three unit citations with the other members of his firehouse.

His wife, Maryann, once asked him if, before running into a burning building or attempting a hazardous rescue, he ever stopped to think about the fact that he had a wife and two children waiting for him at home. "If we did that," Kevin told her, "we'd all be standing outside saying, 'You go ahead, I'll wait here.' You can't think like that."

Kevin's family knew he was doing something he loved and had dreamed about since he was a boy. Just prior to September 11 a television crew was following the work of Kevin's rescue unit and they asked him why he became a firefighter. "I guess it goes back many years to when I was a kid," he said. "The apartment building I lived in, we had—over the years I was there—ended up having three different fires, so I was carried out as a child by . . . by a firefighter. So I have fond memories—you know, I have memories to go back to, you know, all of a sudden, you know, in the smoke, this big guy comes up, grabs me, and carries me down the stairs."

Hannah knew Kevin wanted to be that sort of role model for kids as well. At his station house in downtown Brooklyn, all the kids in the neighborhood knew they could come by and ask for help if their bikes were broken. Flat tires, busted chains, squeaky brakes—Kevin was always glad to make repairs. His fellow firefighters even hung a sign on his locker: KEVIN'S BIKE SHOP.

Hannah thought about all of this and more as she waited on the plane. It was all she could do—think back on the past and pray for the future.

∎

George Vitale was reading the textbook for his sociology of education class that night at Brooklyn College, when the captain for Continental Flight 23 made an announcement.

"There is a report of a terrorist strike," the captain declared.

As the captain allowed the words to sink in, Vitale was unconcerned. He assumed it must have been something routine, like a bomb scare at Newark Airport, where they were scheduled to land. He started thinking about what he would do if the plane was diverted to JFK.

"It's been confirmed," the pilot continued, "that two planes have struck the World Trade Center and a third plane or a bomb has hit the Pentagon."

Gasps echoed through the plane.

"They've shut down the airspace over the United States. We've been ordered by the U.S. government to get on the ground immediately. Our plane is okay. There is nothing wrong with our plane. We're going to be landing at an airport in Gander, Newfoundland. I'm going to be busy, so I'll talk to you when we land. We'll be on the ground in fifteen minutes."

Patty!

Vitale's mind immediately went to his sister Patty, who worked at an insurance company inside the Trade Center's South Tower. She'd lost her husband to pulmonary fibrosis a little more than a year ago and now she might be dead as well. He thought about his fourteen-year-old nephew, Patrick. Vitale was the boy's guardian.

If the unthinkable did happen to Patty, he'd have to raise Patrick by himself. Vitale wondered if he was capable of raising a child, especially a teenager. He worried about living up to the promises he'd made to his sister.

Vitale was amazed at how many things could run through his mind simultaneously. If he was going to care for his nephew, he'd have to move to New Jersey. After all, he wouldn't want to pull the boy out of his school or away from his friends. Not now. Not after having gone through so much. But if Vitale moved to New Jersey, he'd have to leave his job with the New York State Police. Maybe he could keep a mailing address in Brooklyn. Or maybe he could get a waiver from the rule of having to live in the state.

As he spiraled through worst-case scenarios, the plane landed in Gander. Vitale flagged down one of the flight attendants and asked her to take the captain his business card, which identified him as a New York State trooper. On the back of the card, Vitale wrote: "If I can be of any assistance, I'm in seat 16C."

A few minutes later the flight attendant came back and told Vitale the captain would like to see him. The captain seemed as confused and mystified as everyone else. How could this have happened? What should they do? What were they up against? No one had answers.

Vitale was traveling with three telephones. His own cell phone and two government-issued "world phones," which he was assured by his commanders would work anywhere on the planet.

The world phones, however, didn't work in Gander. Vitale wondered if their failure had to do with the reliability of the phones or with the location of the town. Were they truly in the middle of nowhere?

Sitting inside the cockpit, he tried to get a dial tone on his regular cell phone. Every time he dialed a number in the United States, a local operator came on the line. For reasons he couldn't understand, the operator told him the only calls he could make would be through her and only to toll-free numbers. Using the operator, he placed a call to the trooper station at the governor's mansion in Albany. He asked the trooper who answered for a favor. Would he please call his family and see if they were all right and if any of them had heard from Patty? Vitale also asked if he would call the pilot's wife in Houston and ask her to notify the families of the other crew members and let them know they were safe and on the ground in Newfoundland.

"No problem," the trooper said.

Finally he asked the trooper to patch him through to the governor's office in New York City. Vitale had worked for Pataki since he came into office and he liked him a great deal. Vitale first joined the New York State Police in 1981. From 1989 until 1993, he investigated organized crime cases and worked undercover infiltrating the Bonanno crime family. As a result of his work, dozens of mafiosi had gone to prison. Since then he's been responsible for coordinating the governor's security detail when the governor came to New York City.

Until 1996, the governor's Manhattan offices were on the fifty-seventh floor of the World Trade Center's South Tower. Vitale went to work there every day and still knew a lot of people in the building.

After a few minutes, Vitale was connected to the governor's office on East Fortieth Street and Third Avenue, about three and a half miles from the towers.

"Is the governor all right?" Vitale asked. "Where is he?"

The governor was fine. He was downtown with the mayor.

"Are our people okay?" Vitale inquired.

As far as they could tell, no troopers were missing. Everything was still very chaotic, though. Vitale could tell by the tone of the other man's voice that he was scared, which made Vitale more anxious. He began feeling guilty that he wasn't in New York to help out.

▌

As he prepared to make his final approach into Gander, Captain Reinhard Knoth told the passengers that problems in the United States were forcing them to land in Canada. He didn't tell them what those problems were.

Twenty minutes later they were on the ground. It was around 1 P.M. Newfoundland time, and Knoth marveled at all of the airplanes he saw lining the taxiways. For the first time in hours, he felt a sense of relief. He was on the ground. His plane and passengers were safe.

Hugo Boss chairman Werner Baldessarini wondered what type of problems in the United States could have forced them to land in Canada. More important, he wanted to know when they would be leaving. He had a lot riding on this year's fashion show and he needed to be in New York.

Once on the ground, Baldessarini had his answer. Knoth explained the situation in New York and Washington. He also noted that they had just received word of a fourth plane having crashed in Pennsylvania. Thousands were feared dead. Baldessarini felt ashamed for worrying about his fashion show. Fashion Week now seemed so trivial. How quickly a person's priorities could shift, he thought.

Frankfurt mayor Petra Roth worried about her own city. Naturally she was heartbroken over events in the United States, but if American cities were under attack, then European cities might be next.

∎

*L*adies and gentlemen, this is Captain Bass. We've been advised there has been a national emergency in the United States. All of the airspace has been closed and we will be landing our airplane in Gander, Newfoundland."

American Airlines Flight 49, en route from Paris to Dallas, was one of the last planes to approach Gander. On board U.S. Army brigadier general Barbara Fast heard the pilot's announcement and immediately reached for the plane's sky phone. The director of intelligence for the United States military command, Fast oversaw the military's information and spy gathering in ninety-one countries throughout Europe, Africa, and the Middle East.

Based in the German city of Stuttgart, Fast had been in Paris meeting with French officials and was on her way to the U.S. Army Intelligence Center at Fort Huachuca in Arizona when the pilot advised everyone that the plane would be landing in Gander. Replaying the pilot's words in her mind, General Fast focused on the term "national emergency." Clearly, something dire was happening in the United States.

Initially, some passengers worried that the plane had been hijacked and the pilot's announcement was a ruse to explain their change in course. Fast knew better. She was sitting toward the front of the plane, in coach, and hadn't seen any unusual movements or disturbances that would indicate a hijacking. Instead she suspected some form of a terrorist activity in the United States. She wondered if there had been an attempt on the president's life or an attack on a specific target, like the White House or the Capitol.

Anticipating and trying to uncover the plans of known terrorist groups is a major responsibility for Fast and her command staff. She wanted to reach them, to learn what was happening. The sky phones, however, were not working, and it was almost forty-five minutes before they finally landed in Gander. Once on the ground, she tried using her cell phone, but to no avail. As is customary, Fast was traveling in civilian clothing, so no one on the plane knew who she was. Through the flight attendants, she contacted the pilot and reveal her identity and the importance of her being able to reach her staff. There was little the pilot could do.

Fast kept trying the sky phones until she was able to place a call back to Germany. Her aides briefed her on the attack.

Planes had crashed into the towers, the Pentagon, and a field in Pennsylvania. More planes were assumed missing.

There was no doubt in the general's mind as to who was responsible for this cowardly act: Osama bin Laden. The Saudi millionaire was one of the few people in the world who would have the resources and the organization to accomplish such a deed. His war against the United States had been escalating in recent years, and he was believed to be responsible for the 1998 bombings of the U.S. embassies in Kenya and Tanzania, and the October 2000 attack on the USS *Cole* in the Yemeni port of Aden. Now, it appeared, he was bringing his jihad to American shores.

The first priority for Fast, who had been intelligence chief only since June, was to make sure everything was being done to guarantee the safety of U.S. military personnel in the various countries under her watch. She feared the attacks in New York and Washington could be only the first wave in a series of terrorist strikes against Americans around the world. Securing American military bases is easy enough, but she was concerned about housing complexes and other facilities off base where Americans might be gathered. As she expected, when she was finally able to call the command center, her staff was already coordinating efforts with local officials in each country.

The second priority was obviously to uncover any information available about the planning for these attacks so it could be passed along to Washington. Fast and her staff were limited in their discussions by the fact they were not on a secure phone line. Her cell phone, which eventually worked, was also unsecured. She needed to get off the plane and begin making plans for her return to Stuttgart as soon as possible.

Captain Beverley Bass, the American Airlines pilot, sympathized with Fast's plight. The pilot tried relaying the urgency of the situation to airport officials in Gander, but the situation on the ground was so chaotic there was nothing they could do.

No one was going to get off any of the planes until the RCMP could secure the airport and find a way to process all of the passengers to guarantee they wouldn't mistakenly let a terrorist slip through their grasp.

Fast could do nothing but sit and wait along with everyone else. And since her plane was one of the last to arrive in Gander, its passengers would be among the last to be processed. The waiting gave her time to think. The day's events filled her with shock and anger. Understandably, she wondered what was happening at the Pentagon. She worried how the attack was affecting the military's ability to coordinate the country's defenses against further assault. And on a personal level, she wondered how many of her friends in the building were missing or dead.

CHAPTER FOUR

Gander International Airport, September 11, 2001.

The succession of jet engines roaring over town caused people to come out of their homes and businesses to watch the line of planes in the sky. The arrival of the diverted aircraft in Gander quickly replaced the weather as the main topic of conversation. Not since World War II had the airport seen this much activity. Hundreds of people drove out to watch. Their cars clogged the access roads circling the airport as they stopped to take pictures of the different types of planes from so many different airlines. Virgin Air. British Airways. Air Italia. Air France. Sabena. Lufthansa. Aer Lingus. TWA. Delta. Continental. American. US Air. Northwest. Air Hungaria. The list went on and on.

There were military planes and a few private jets as well. There were so many planes, in fact, that airport officials had to use Gander's second runway as a parking lot for some of them. The planes were stacked, nose to tail, one after another.

Lining the fences around the airport, people just stood by their cars waving to the passengers on board. On a few of the planes, the doors were opened for ventilation and to lessen the feeling of claustrophobia among the passengers. There were no stairs and the only way off was to jump about twenty feet to the ground, but the open doorway gave the townspeople a chance to shout hello to anyone who passed by.

Inside the airport Geoff Tucker was worrying about the logistics of having more than three dozen planes on the ground. Even if the passengers never set foot off of the planes, the aircraft were all going to need to be serviced with fuel. The toilets on the planes would have to be emptied before they started overflowing. And the planes might have to be restocked with supplies of food and water.

As Tucker started addressing these problems, in the back of his mind he believed these planes were going to be grounded for more than just a short delay since it didn't seem likely that airspace over the United States would open up again soon. Eventually, he thought to himself, the town was going to have to find a place for all of these people.

Mayor Elliott had the same concern. There were only two groups in town that had the training and expertise to handle such a crisis: the local chapters of the Red Cross and the Salvation Army. The heads of both organizations were placed on alert.

▮

While Geoff Tucker was organizing things at Gander International Airport and Mayor Elliott was mobilizing aid organizations and members of the community in an effort to foresee the needs of the stranded passengers, an unanticipated problem arose almost immediately and needed a quick solution. Not long after the planes started landing, airport officials began receiving desperate pleas for help from many of the captains. A growing number of their passengers were climbing the cabin walls for a cigarette. Mentally these smokers had braced themselves for a six-hour transatlantic flight without any tobacco. But as their time on board the aircraft suddenly became indefinite and their stress levels skyrocketed as they tried to comprehend the severity of the situation that had brought them to Gander, the nicotine "jones" began to grip them something fierce.

A few flight crews broke the rules and allowed small groups of passengers to light up near the open door of the plane. Most, however, enforced the no-smoking mandate. On one Continental flight, two passengers needed to be sedated because they developed the shakes so bad.

The problem of how to handle these smokers was passed along to the Red Cross's Dave Dillon. It was his idea to call Kevin O'Brien, owner of MediPlus Pharmacy.

"Kevin, I don't know what you can do for me, but we've got people stuck on the aircrafts and we've got a problem," he explained.

O'Brien isn't a smoker, but he certainly could sympathize with the plight of those who were. He grabbed several empty boxes and cleaned out his entire supply of nicotine gum. He then filled the backseat of his car with twenty-five cartons of nicotine patches. In the United States a person needs a pre-scription before he can obtain the nicotine patch, but in Canada they are sold over the counter. O'Brien raced down to the airport, where Mounties delivered the items to each of the planes requesting them.

I

Geoff Tucker had a new problem that was beginning to scare him. After all of the planes landed, tower officials made the rounds by radio, talking to each of the pilots to let them know what was happening. Five of the airplanes, however, weren't responding to hails on their radio. The tower had alerted Tucker and he had a bad feeling. What if these five pilots weren't responding because something awful was happening on their planes? The RCMP and the military had so effectively drummed into his head the possibility that there were terrorists aboard these planes that Tucker started to think it was true.

Complicating matters further, the tower couldn't determine which five of the thirty-eight planes on the ground were the ones not responding. They knew the airlines and flight numbers, but they didn't have the corresponding tail numbers. The airport's command post is a large room with a horseshoe-shaped table. Each of the major agencies has a spot at the table. Talking to the controllers in the tower and duty managers on the tarmac, Tucker could tell that both the RCMP chief and the air-force base commander were following his conversation with interest.

Tucker also realized that because the parked planes were all bunched together, an explosion on one of the planes would probably destroy all of the ones around it as well, in a virtual chain reaction. Not wanting to sound alarmist, Tucker suggested that his ground crews might want to try to find those missing planes as soon as possible.

▌

By mid-afternoon it was obvious that U.S. airspace was going to remain closed for the foreseeable future. When the word officially arrived from the FAA, town leaders were already establishing shelters for as many as 12,000 people. The schools were the most obvious place to start.

Terry Andrews received the call just before classes were to be let out for the day at St. Paul's Intermediate, the town's junior high school. As the principal, he went on the PA system and instructed all of the students to clean out their desks, since they were going to have to fill up the classrooms with cots. Similar messages were being delivered at the high school, Gander Collegiate, and the elementary school, Gander Academy.

All of the churches in town were placed on notice, as well as the fraternal organizations such as the Lions Club, the Knights of Columbus, and the Royal Canadian Legion hall.

Without waiting to be asked, the mayors from the smaller surrounding towns started calling in, offering their own facilities for passengers. The Salvation Army not only had churches in several of these towns, but they also had a summer camp, out in the woods, which could hold hundreds of people.

The air force base, 9 Gander Wing, was already on alert. All of its airmen and reserves were called in and the officers' club was quickly converted into a shelter.

One place where passengers wouldn't stay was in any of the town's 550 hotel rooms. Soon after the planes landed, Geoff Tucker realized he needed to make sure the flight crews had a decent place to stay. Pilots and flight attendants are required to have a certain amount of rest or they are not allowed to fly. Tucker estimated there to be 500 pilots, copilots, flight engineers, pursers, and flight attendants aboard the planes. Tucker called town manager Jake Turner.

"We're going to need every hotel room in town," the airport vice-president told him. "You are going to have to seize all of the rooms and force the hotels to cancel any existing reservations they have."

"I can't do that unless the town council declares a state of emergency," Turner replied.

"Well, then, I guess you need to declare a state of emergency," Tucker said. He explained the situation to Turner. Within two hours the town council met and declared that a state of emergency was now in effect. Tucker's instincts were right. A number of quick-thinking passengers had already used their cell phones to call local hotels and book blocks of rooms with their credit cards. Once the state of emergency was declared, all of those reservations were canceled.

Tucker soon discovered another crisis that had been averted. After visiting each of the planes personally, his ground managers reported that all of the planes had been accounted for, including the five planes that failed to respond to radio hails earlier. Some of the pilots had either shut down their radios to conserve power or were monitoring a different frequency when the tower called. Tucker let out a sigh of relief when he heard the news. Finally, he thought to himself, things were starting to look up.

▌

Moving the passengers off the plane was going to be complicated. The first issue was security. In order to ensure everyone's safety, officials would deal with only one plane at a time, in the order in which they landed. After getting off the plane, the passengers would run through a gauntlet of security. They would go through metal detectors as well as being patted down. Then their carry-on bags would be emptied and searched. All of the luggage they checked onto the plane before departing would stay in the belly of the plane.

After clearing security, they would proceed through customs and immigration. This was complicated by the fact that only one immigration agent had been assigned to Gander, Murray Osmond. Help was on the way from St. John's, but in the beginning at least, Osmond was on his own.

From there the passengers were turned over to the Canadian Red Cross and Des Dillon. A retired government employee, Dillon had been involved with the relief agency for thirty years and was specially trained as a disaster coordinator. In 1994, he was sent to Los Angeles following the devastating Northridge earthquake, which killed fifty-seven people. He supervised more than two thousand volunteers during that catastrophe. He had also helped coordinate relief efforts after the 1998 Swiss Air crash off the coast of Nova Scotia. The Red Cross would register each and every passenger and keep track of which shelter they were assigned to. Within a couple of hours Dillon had two hundred volunteers at the airport. He wanted to move the passengers through the airport as fast as possible so that those on the next plane could be taken off. He made sure all of the television sets in the airport were either hidden or unplugged. He knew the passengers hadn't seen any of the images of the attack and was afraid they would emotionally break down in the terminal. To keep them moving, Out of Order signs were posted on all of the pay phones in the airport. The phones actually worked, but officials were afraid people would stop and wait in line to call their homes.

The biggest problem facing officials was transportation. How do you move almost 7,000 people to shelters, some of which were almost fifty miles outside of town? The logical answer was to use school buses. On September 11, however, Gander was in the midst of a nasty strike by the area's school-bus drivers.

Amazingly, as soon as the drivers realized what was happening, they laid down their picket signs, setting their own interests aside, and volunteered en masse to work around the clock carrying the passengers wherever they needed to go.

In town, the Salvation Army was in charge of gathering supplies and acting as a central clearinghouse for the shelters. The local radio station and public-access television station started running announcements asking folks in town to donate food, spare bedding, old clothes—anything the passengers might need. At the town's community center, a line of cars stretched from the front door for two miles as people brought sheets and blankets and pillows from their homes for the passengers.

Local stores donated thousands of dollars' worth of items. O'Brien, the pharmacist, coordinated with all of the other pharmacies in the area to supply all of the toiletries the unexpected arrivals might need, including a special shipment of 4,000 toothbrushes.

∎

Once all 252 of the planes diverted to Canada were safely on the ground and it was clear that none of them would be taking off again, Dwayne Puddister left Gander's air-traffic control center, picked up a steak and some beer, and headed over to the home of fellow controller Keith Mills. Soon a half-dozen other controllers from the center arrived for a celebratory barbecue.

None of them had ever been through a day like this. They

were all so relieved it was over that none of them wanted to be alone. The closest thing Puddister could liken it to was driving on icy roads through a blinding snowstorm; both hands on the steering wheel, knuckles white, and hypersensitive to everything, you don't realize how scared you are until you pull into the driveway. In the morning, Puddister would help unload supply trucks at one of the local community centers that had taken in passengers. Tonight, however, he'd have a thick steak and a few bottles of Canadian ale.

Reg Batson finished his shift at the ATC and went to the town's Masonic temple. A longtime Mason, he helped prepare for the arrival of ninety-one passengers from TWA Flight 819 out of Paris and offered his home to any passenger needing a shower.

By the end of the day, Harold O'Reilly wasn't sure what to do about his fiftieth birthday. He didn't feel much like going out. But at the same time, turning fifty was a big deal. As he drove home, he was preparing himself for some sort of celebration, maybe a banner across the front door saying HAPPY BIRTHDAY from his family. He knew his wife had been busy all day volunteering around town, but still, he thought, she might try to surprise him by inviting some of their friends over for a drink and a piece of birthday cake. When he arrived home the house was quiet. No banner. No friends. No cake. In all the commotion of the day, everyone, including his wife, had forgotten it was Harold's birthday.

CHAPTER FIVE

Setting up at the Lions Club.

Roxanne Loper felt like a woman without a time zone. Her body was on Moscow time. Her watch was on Dallas time. And her fears were working overtime. She knew when they had left Russia, and she knew when they were due into Dallas, but she couldn't quite figure out what time it was in Gander. All she knew for sure was that she had been on this plane for what seemed like an eternity.

Two hours after being diverted to Newfoundland, she still didn't know why airspace over the United States had been closed. The pilot had offered no additional information and none of the phones on the plane worked, not even individuals' cell phones. Roxanne's immediate concern was getting in touch with her family. She wanted them to know that she and Clark and Alexandria were safe.

Flight attendants told passengers to conserve food and water since they didn't know how long they would be on the ground. By midafternoon, one of the sky phones on the plane was suddenly working. Since Roxanne was sitting closest to the phone, she made the first call. She tried her parents' house. No answer. Her in-laws' house. No answer. Her brother's house. Again, no answer. She left messages on their answering machines.

"We're in Canada," she said, being careful not to let her voice intimate just how scared she was. "We don't know when we are going to get out of here. Don't worry, we're all okay."

As other passengers used the phone, word began spreading through the plane about what was happening in the United States.

Have you heard? Seven planes hijacked! The towers of the Trade Center have collapsed! The Pentagon and the White House have been hit! More than 10,000 people are dead! The president has gone into a hidden nuclear bunker!

Some of the stories were true and many others were false. They all seemed unbelievable.

A few rows away from Roxanne and Clark, Lisa Cox was hearing the same wild stories. The eighteen-year-old was flying home with her mother and sister after spending eleven days in Italy, courtesy of the Children's Wish Foundation. When she was sixteen years old, Cox's doctors discovered a tumor growing inside her and determined she had ovarian cancer. Since then she'd undergone surgery to remove her ovaries and chemotherapy.

During her treatments, she applied for a wish through the

foundation and was granted one. Her first request was to meet singer Mariah Carey. She was a huge fan of the pop diva. The biggest. Unfortunately, her timing wasn't very good and her request coincided with the time when Mariah was suffering a nervous breakdown.

The foundation told Cox to make another request. A friend had once told her how beautiful Italy was, so she thought a trip to the country with her mother and older sister was good idea. There would at least be lots of shopping. They went to Venice and Florence and the Isle of Capri near Naples, and then on to Rome.

Oh my God, we're at war, Cox thought to herself on the plane in Gander.

Her mother, Betty Schmidt, had another thought. What if terrorists were planning on taking over this plane when it reached the United States? There could be frustrated terrorists on the plane right now. She didn't say anything to her daughters, but as she walked down the aisle to stretch her legs, she couldn't help but study her fellow passengers. What does a terrorist look like? She didn't know how to answer that question.

▌

At 4:30 P.M., the passengers aboard Virgin Air Flight 75, the first plane to land in Gander, made their way off the plane and into the terminal. It took almost three hours for the 337 passengers to go through the various checkpoints and board buses for the shelter. At that rate it would take almost three days to get all of the passengers off the planes. Des Dillon wasn't worried, however. He knew the first plane would take some time while each of the agencies perfected the way they did things and added more staff.

Before long, they would be able to process a plane every forty-five minutes. For now, though, it was a slow and arduous task.

Watching the passengers as they moved through the terminal, Dillon was amazed by their demeanor. No one was cranky or complaining. They all seemed in good spirits. Without any TVs or telephones to distract the passengers, there weren't any unnecessary delays. Except for one.

A volunteer had taped a large map of the world to the wall and with a crude red marker drew an arrow pointing to Gander. You ARE HERE, the volunteer wrote on the map. Exhausted passengers would stop and stare at the map for several minutes, trying to regain their bearings.

❙

After more than seven hours on the ground, the passengers aboard Lufthansa Flight 438 were allowed to get off the plane. It was about 8:30 P.M. local time when a portable staircase was pushed against the plane and everyone filed off. Since they had been one of the first planes on the ground, they were close enough to the terminal to walk the fifty or so yards to the entrance.

The sweet smell of the night air was the first thing Roxanne Loper noticed. The doors on the plane had been kept closed while they were on the ground and the air inside had grown stale. On her way off the plane, Roxanne grabbed a couple of blankets and some pillows out of first class. She assumed the passengers would have to camp out somewhere inside the airport until their flight was ready to leave. They might even have to sleep there.

Once they cleared security and customs, passengers were

told to walk down a corridor to the main terminal. The airport seemed eerily empty and quiet and she had no idea where she was going. As she reached the end of the corridor, Roxanne started to hear the sound of people ahead. Turning the corner, she was greeted by a phalanx of strangers waving her toward tables manned by folks in red-and-white vests and windbreakers.

"Oh my God, it's the Red Cross," she said.

The sight of dozens of Red Cross volunteers was jarring. The relief agency helps earthquake survivors, she thought to herself, people who lose their home in hurricanes and tornadoes and floods. It's for victims of tragedy. That wasn't her. Was it? She wondered if this meant she and her family were somehow viewed as "victims" of the terrorist attacks. She didn't like thinking of herself as a victim.

One thing was certain. If the Red Cross had been mobilized, then this wasn't going to be a delay of only a few hours. They were going to be here a while. Several volunteers immediately approached Roxanne and Clark and asked if they needed anything special for Alexandria.

"Diapers," Roxanne said.

"What size?" one of the volunteers asked before rushing off.

The couple were handed bags containing a sandwich, a slice of pizza, and bottled water and ushered to a table, where they were asked their name and phone number. Roxanne still had no idea what was going to happen to them. Smiling people just kept directing them from one point to the next until finally she found herself standing outside the airport.

"Please, get on the bus," a man said, motioning to one of the yellow school buses in the parking lot. "Everyone, please get on the bus."

There was an entire fleet of yellow school buses waiting for passengers. Once one was filled, the next one pulled up. It wasn't until they were boarding the bus that Roxanne and Clark learned that the passengers from her flight were being evacuated to the Lions Club. Once everyone from her flight was aboard buses, the caravan moved out. Driving down the dark road from the airport into Gander, Roxanne stared out the window, trying to get her bearings. Along the main road through town, she spotted a number of familiar landmarks that made her feel welcome. McDonald's. Kentucky Fried Chicken. And perhaps most reassuring of all, a giant Wal-Mart.

The Gander Lions Club has forty-seven members and a building it shares with the local senior citizens' group. It has its own bar for special events and a complete kitchen with a double-size commercial stove, large griddle, and twin ovens.

Pulling up to the Lions Club, the buses were greeted by a dozen people all waving and smiling and calling out, "How she goin', buddy?" Roxanne and Clark soon learned that when Newfies don't know a person's name, they just call that person "buddy."

Inside the Lions Club, most passengers spilled into the hall's main room. Bruce MacLeod intercepted Roxanne and Clark as they walked in. A tall gregarious fellow with graying hair and a broad smile, MacLeod was the vice-president of the club. At 8 A.M. he had finished his shift monitoring radar at the air-traffic control center and was getting ready to go to sleep when he learned about the attack in the United States and the diverted flights. He called in to the ATC to see if he was needed, but they already had enough volunteers. Instead, along with most of the other members of the club, he worked all afternoon readying the place for passengers.

"We need to put you in a separate room since you have a

child," MacLeod told Roxanne and Clark. He showed them to smaller room where a half-dozen families with children would stay. Beth and Billy Wakefield—the other couple who'd adopted a baby in Kazakhstan—were already inside with Diana. There were air mattresses and sleeping bags piled high in the room, and before long nearly every inch of the floor would be covered by them.

Roxanne and Clark lay down on one mattress, with Alexandria between them. The child fell asleep almost immediately. While Clark stayed on the air mattress with Alexandria, Roxanne decided to clean up and explore the Lions Club. In the bathroom she found a bucket filled with packages of new toothbrushes. In another bucket, she found every imaginable brand of toothpaste. Also inside the bathroom was a mountain of neatly folded towels. There were hand towels and bath towels in a variety of colors and patterns, which made Roxanne realize every member of the club must have emptied his home closet to meet the need.

After washing up, she walked into the hall's main room, which was surprisingly quiet, except for the sound coming from the television. The TV set was to Roxanne's immediate right, mounted on the wall, and pointing away from her, so she couldn't tell what was on the screen. But she could see the faces of the people watching it. Their expressions made her stop. Mouths slightly agape. Eyes wide. And although nobody was crying outright, a few seemed teary. The stillness chilled her. No one talked. No one whispered. And no one looked away. Some people had their arms folded, like they were trying to hold themselves for comfort. Others held their heads in their hands.

Instantly Roxanne realized the scenes from New York were worse than she imagined. Perhaps even worse than she was capable of imagining. She thought about turning around and walking out of the room. Did she really need to see this tonight? Besides, maybe people were reacting as they were because they were tired. Maybe the images wouldn't seem so bad after a good night's rest. But how could she possibly sleep now? She decided it was better to get it over with.

Slowly, almost tiptoeing, she continued into the room, casting a small arc to the back of the crowd. Looking up, she saw the live reports from the rubble of the towers. At that moment she, too, became transfixed, mouth slightly agape, eyes wide and watery.

Roxanne had never been to New York, but she'd always wanted to go. Now, she thought, so much of it will never be the same again. It wasn't long before she saw a replay of the planes—big commercial airliners like the one she'd boarded that morning—crashing into the buildings, creating orange fireballs. Finally she watched as each tower caved in on itself.

She watched for almost an hour. Numbed by the repetition. Although standing in a crowd, she didn't want to be alone anymore. She went back to the family room and sat down on the mattress next to Clark.

"It's bad," she said. "You should go see."

Clark stood and walked into the main room. Shock quickly gave way to anger as he watched CNN. Why would someone do this? Who would want to kill so many innocent people? The more he watched, the angrier he became until finally he knew he shouldn't watch any longer. In the family room one of the babies was crying. He crawled into bed alongside Alexandria and Roxanne and closed his eyes. He wanted to go to sleep. He wanted this day to be over.

▌

Finally some good news. After several hours, New York State trooper George Vitale received word that his sister was alive.

At first he didn't quite believe it. He wondered if the trooper in Albany who passed along the information had somehow made a mistake and confused Patty with Vitale's other sister.

"Are you sure it was Patty you spoke to?" Vitale asked the trooper.

"Yes," the trooper insisted. Through an odd twist of fate, Patty was shopping in one of the stores under the World Trade Center when the first plane hit, and she immediately left the area. Vitale was relieved. He also felt a bit silly for all the plans he was mentally making to raise his nephew under the assumption that Patty might be dead.

As time passed, Vitale continued to receive only snippets of information. Officials at the airport weren't providing any updates, nor were the air-traffic controllers. The pilot even told Vitale the plane's radio was useless. They needed to be in the air for the captain to call back to Continental's home base in Houston to find out what was happening. And he assumed that any attempts to pick up a commercial radio station while they were sitting on the tarmac would be futile.

Most of the information passengers had gathered came from the brief telephone calls they were making to family members. Rumors began circulating that both towers had collapsed. Vitale didn't think this was possible. Then he finally discovered it was true. Worse still, there were scores of fire-fighters and police officers in the buildings at the time.

Vitale had a new worry. His best friend through high school, Anthony DeRubbio, was a New York City firefighter. For that matter, virtually the entire DeRubbio family was made up of firefighters. Three of Anthony's brothers—Dominick, Robert, and David—were in the FDNY. Vitale's thoughts were with Anthony. They were the same age and had gone to the same schools—St. Agatha's Elementary in Brooklyn and Aviation High School in Queens. The reason Vitale went to Aviation was that it was where Anthony wanted to go. Their birthdays were just six days apart. Vitale was born on September 19. Anthony's birthday was September 25. When they were kids, Vitale would never let Anthony forget that he was older. Could Anthony really be gone?

During the flight, Tom McKeon was sitting in the row just ahead of Vitale, and the two men started talking soon after landing. When Vitale told McKeon he was positive the towers had collapsed, McKeon was just as certain Vitale must be mistaken.

Vitale lent McKeon his phone so he could call his father. McKeon's father was a firefighter for thirty-five years in West New York, a town just across the Hudson River in New Jersey. There wasn't a place in town from which you couldn't see the towers.

"Are the towers really gone?" McKeon asked his father.

"They're all gone," he said.

"And the firefighters?"

"Yeah," his father said mournfully.

Hearing it from his father was the first time McKeon believed the unimaginable had happened.

▮

Moving around the plane, Vitale had an idea. He was a talk-radio junkie who loved listening to the stations in the city. The pilot was probably right; parked on the ground, they couldn't pick up most commercial radio stations, but Vitale knew 770 AM, WABC, had a particularly strong signal and at night could be heard as far away as Maine.

Maybe tonight they'd be able to pick it up in Newfoundland.

The pilot, Tom Carroll, was willing to try and gingerly

played with the dials on the receiver. The copilot was seated next to him and several flight attendants were also in the cockpit, as was Vitale. Carroll could feel their eyes staring at him as he tried to locate the right frequency. At first all he could find was static, but when he struck upon the New York station, a small cheer erupted in the cockpit. Before the celebration went too far, they were floored by the words spilling out of the speakers. Thousands, maybe tens of thousands, were thought to be dead. For hours they remained glued to the radio.

At 10 P.M. in Gander, Vitale, the pilot, and the crew huddled in the dimly lit cockpit and listened to the president's address to the nation.

> *Good evening. Today, our fellow citizens, our way of life, our very freedom came under attack in a series of deliberate and deadly terrorist acts. The victims were in airplanes or in their offices; secretaries, businessmen and women, military and federal workers; moms and dads, friends and neighbors. Thousands of lives were suddenly ended by evil, despicable acts of terror.*

> *The pictures of airplanes flying into buildings, fires burning, huge structures collapsing, have filled us with disbelief, terrible sadness, and a quiet, unyielding anger. These acts of mass murder were intended to frighten our nation into chaos and retreat. But they have failed; our country is strong.*

> *A great people has been moved to defend a great nation. Terrorist attacks can shake the foundations of our biggest buildings, but they cannot touch the foundation of America. These acts shattered steel, but they cannot dent the steel of American resolve . . .*

Listening to the president's speech, Vitale was in a state of shock. How could this be happening? he thought to himself. How could somebody do this? Staring out the pilot's window, he looked across a darkened airfield, which only added to his sense of isolation. He felt overwhelmed. Tears welled up in his eyes.

America was targeted for attack because we're the brightest beacon for freedom and opportunity in the world. And no one will keep that light from shining.

Today, our nation saw evil, the very worst of human nature. And we responded with the best of America—with the daring of our rescue workers, with the caring for strangers and neighbors who came to give blood and help in any way they could . . .

Standing in the doorway of the cockpit was McKeon. As the president spoke, he couldn't help but imagine that this must have been what it was like for his parents and grandparents during World War II. Gathered around a radio, learning about the attack on Pearl Harbor, and then listening to the president, searching for hope and strength in his words.

The search is under way for those who are behind these evil acts. I've directed the full resources of our intelligence and law enforcement communities to find those responsible and to bring them to justice. We will make no distinction between the terrorists who committed these acts and those who harbor them . . .

Tonight, I ask for your prayers for all those who grieve, for the children whose worlds have been shattered, for all

*whose sense of safety and security has been threatened.
And I pray they will be comforted by a power greater than
any of us, spoken through the ages in Psalm 23: "Even
though I walk through the valley of the shadow of death, I
fear no evil, for You are with me."*

*This is a day when all Americans from every walk of life
unite in our resolve for justice and peace. America has
stood down enemies before, and we will do so this time.
None of us will ever forget this day. Yet we go forward to
defend freedom and all that is good and just in our world.*

Thank you. Good night, and God bless America.

The cockpit fell silent when the president concluded.
Vitale's face was flushed and he could feel the tears on his
cheeks. He was embarrassed by his reaction and quickly composed himself before anyone could notice. As a police officer,
he worried that people would be looking to him to show
strength and he didn't want to show any sign of weakness.
Wiping away the tears, he was filled with another emotion.
Pride. At that moment he had never been more proud to be an
American.

❚

Ten hours after landing, the 372 passengers and crew members of Lufthansa Flight 400 were allowed to leave the aircraft.
While everyone else boarded buses that would take them to the
terminal for processing, Captain Reinhard Knoth stayed
behind. The RCMP and Canadian military were running the
names of all passengers from each of the planes through vari-

ous intelligence databases and Knoth was told the name of one of his passengers matched up with the name of a suspected terrorist.

Inside the terminal, the man would be quietly pulled aside and detained for questioning by the police. In the meantime, RCMP officials were concerned that the passenger might have hidden something, possibly a bomb, on board the jumbo jet. Knoth believed the police were being a bit overzealous. If a passenger had taken a bomb onto the plane, he would have blown it up by now. Why wait?

The strain of the day's events was evident on the faces of the police surrounding the plane. None of them knew what to expect from one minute to the next. Knoth realized that the moment the first plane hit the first tower, the old rules on combating global terrorism had ceased to apply, but nobody was sure what the new rules would be.

Walking through the empty aircraft, Knoth accompanied a small squad of officers looking for anything suspicious. After going through the area where the man was sitting, they spread throughout the rest of the plane. Excitedly, one of the officers called out that he'd found something in one of the overhead compartments. It was an oddly shaped cylindrical metal container. Knoth walked over and stared at it for a moment.

Moving quickly to call in the bomb squad, the officers backed away from the shiny metal object and told Knoth to do the same. Instead, he stepped forward. Reaching into the overhead bin, Knoth heard the officers yelling at him to stop, but he picked up the item anyway. He knew he'd recognized it from somewhere.

It was a container of Danzka vodka. A premium vodka made in Denmark and packaged in an aluminum bottle. They sell it at the duty-free shop in Frankfurt. The company's slogan: "Danzka, the Unexpected Vodka."

▌

The passengers of Lufthansa Flight 400 were taken to the local high school, Gander Collegiate. Although they arrived at midnight, Frankfurt mayor Petra Roth and Hugo Boss chairman Werner Baldessarini couldn't believe how many people were waiting to greet the passengers. The volunteers handed out toiletries and bedding and made sure everyone knew there was food and water available.

Although her English is only fair, Mayor Roth introduced herself to various people at the school and thanked them for everything they were doing.

The school was still waiting for a supply of cots to arrive. Baldessarini was so tired he decided to make do with what they already had. He took a blanket and a pillow and staked out a small corner of the school's gym floor. He curled up in his cashmere suit and quickly fell asleep.

▌

George Vitale would have loved to be able to sleep. As long as he was on the plane, however, he found sleeping impossible. Vitale was relieved when the pilot, at about 2 A.M., announced it was now their turn to go through Canadian customs.

The combination of sleep deprivation, stress, and the abundance of security made the passengers a bit skittish as they walked through the terminal.

"Welcome to Gander," a woman said to Vitale's fellow passenger Tom McKeon. "Right this way."

McKeon realized his nerves were more than a little frayed when he asked the woman for permission to use the airport's bathroom and she responded by laughing and telling him, "Of course."

Rather than housing the passengers from Continental Flight 23 in Gander, they were sent by bus fifteen miles down the road to Appleton, a beautiful town of seven hundred people on the eastern banks of the Gander River. The first thing McKeon noticed when he walked into the Appleton Community Center was the smell of coffee. He had served six years in the navy, mostly aboard submarines, and there was always something about the smell of a fresh pot of coffee that was reassuring to him. The second thing he noticed was the television. Vitale saw it as well. Even though he knew by now that the towers had been destroyed, he was still paralyzed by the pictures. At first he thought it must have been some sort of computer simulation. As people gathered around, all of them horrified, many crying, he realized it was real footage of the attack. The television remained on all night, flickering like a candle at the far end of the room.

▮

Thanks to a steady stream of U.S. servicemen and their families, who were stationed in the area, the Baptist church in Gander used to be one of the largest congregations in town. Since the American military presence evaporated in the nineties, however, the church has shriveled into one of the town's smallest. There are six families, about thirty people, who regularly attend services, and they share the guidance of a full-time pastor with a town that is more than an hour away. While the number of Baptists in Gander may have declined, it hasn't diminished their sense of community.

As soon as the first plane landed, Gary House, a church deacon, was on the phone to the town's command center, offering shelter and care for as many of the stranded passengers as could fit inside the church. A retired schoolteacher, House estimated they could comfortably accommodate between thirty and forty people. Since the Baptists weren't in a position to handle a large number of passengers, Red Cross officials delivered them a small but challenging group.

Among the 135 passengers on Delta Flight 141 from Brussels to New York were thirty-eight refugees from Moldova, a part of the former Soviet Union located just east of Romania. The refugees constituted five different families who were being relocated to the United States to start new lives. Three of the women in the group were pregnant. And among the five families there were more than a dozen children—from infants to teenagers.

Communicating with them was going to be difficult since no one in the church spoke Russian. As for the refugees, only one of them, a seventeen-year-old girl who was pregnant and traveling with her husband and her in-laws, spoke a little English. She told the folks in Gander to call her Alice, because she didn't think they would understand her real name, Olesya Buntylo.

Buntylo is a bright young woman with dark hair and a round face. She is modest but funny, and deeply religious. Her family had been saving money for years to make the move to the United States, and on September 11 they were on their way to join other members of their family already living in Renton, Washington, just outside of Seattle. Olesya and her husband, Valeriy, wanted their little girl to be born in a country where religious freedom was well established and she wouldn't be persecuted for being Christian. Although it was now considered a free and independent state, Moldova had not shed all of its old hard-line Communist influences when it came to religion.

Inside the Baptist church, volunteers had arranged the pews into five large squares—almost like mini-forts—which would act as the living quarters for each of the families. They also brought blankets and pillows from their homes, clothes for the adults and the children, and lots of diapers for the babies.

Clark Piercey had some sense of how disorienting it must have been for these people. He knew what it was like to be in a country where you didn't understand the language. He and his wife, Laura, had once been teachers with Canadian Baptist Missionaries and spent six months in Zaire in late 1990. At least they knew in advance what they were getting themselves into and had had time to prepare for it. But he wasn't sure these refugees from the former Soviet Union fully understood what was going on.

Piercey, an air-traffic controller, spent nearly all of his free time at the church. Early on, he brought an atlas from his home to show people where they were. The first night in the church, Piercey volunteered to spend the night with them in case they needed anything. At about two in the morning, one of the men came downstairs to the kitchen in the church basement where Piercey was sitting. The man wanted something, but Piercey couldn't figure it out. Finally, as the man used pointing and hand gestures and little baby noises, Piercey realized the man needed milk to feed one of the babies upstairs. He took out a bottle of formula from the refrigerator and popped it into the microwave. The man grew upset until Piercey handed him the bottle and he realized all Piercey had done was warm it up. It appeared the father had never used a microwave before. It was the start of a long process of discovery for the church members and their unexpected guests. And before it would come to an end, both the Moldovans and the Baptists would become experts in the art of pantomime and charades.

❚

It was nearly 3 A.M. when Newfoundland's long-lost son, Lenny O'Driscoll, disembarked from his plane and set foot on native soil. By the time he and Maria, as well as the other passengers, were processed and bused to the Royal Canadian Legion hall, it was nearing four in the morning. Despite the hour, volunteers were waiting to serve hot soup and fresh sandwiches. The volunteers had been there all night, not sure when their "plane people" would arrive. First they were told to expect them around 6:30 Tuesday evening. Then it was pushed back to ten, and then midnight.

They used the extra time to gather supplies. Beulah Cooper and several of the women from the legion's ladies auxiliary made sandwiches. Cooper mixed up a batch of egg salad as well as a platter of ham-and-cheese sandwiches. The soup was more a hearty stew than a broth, good to ward off any night chills.

Most passengers, though, simply wanted a blanket, a pillow, and a place to lie down. Except for Lenny. He wasn't tired or hungry.

"I want a drink," he declared, slapping his hand down on the legion's long wooden bar, his accent seeming to return with every breath of cool Newfoundland night air. "I've been gone for thirty-five years and I'm back," he continued. "Now, can I get the bar open?"

The president of the legion, Wally Crummell, didn't know what to say. He and the other volunteers had tried to anticipate every contingency and need, from toothpaste to sanitary napkins, but no one had counted on the return of the prodigal Newf.

"Boy, oh boy." Crummell sighed, shaking his head. "We can't open the bar at this hour in the morning. Not with all the young ones around."

Lenny looked around at the children, many of whom were asleep in the arms of their fathers and mothers.

"How about a bottle, then?" Lenny asked. "I'll go sit over there, and anyone who wants to join me for a toast to my return can join me."

Crummell turned to his bar manager, Alf Johnson. The two men decided it would be best to keep the liquor cabinet closed until everyone settled in. Lenny said he understood. He was just excited about being home.

"I'm from South Shore, on the Avalon," Lenny offered, describing a corner of Newfoundland just south of the provincial capital. "That's where all of the O'Driscolls are from."

Crummell knew exactly where Lenny was talking about. There used to be a time when just knowing a fellow's last name gave you a better-than-even chance of telling what town his family came from. As Lenny started reminiscing about his younger days and the Newfoundland of old, Crummell couldn't help but like him.

Lenny was proof positive that no matter how far you travel or how long you stay away, you can take the man out of Newfoundland but you can't take Newfoundland out of the man. Lenny was more than just a character, Crummell thought, he was what folks in the area like to describe as a "real going concern." Crummell could only hope he himself would be as spry and filled with life when he was eighty-two.

"Ah, the heck with it," Crummell privately told Alf Johnson as he pulled him away from Lenny. "As soon as possible, open the bar and give the man a drink."

▌

At the other end of the bar, Hannah O'Rourke waited on line to use the legion's phone so she could call home to learn if there was any news on her son Kevin, the New York City fire-fighter. Despite the hour, she called Kevin's house. His wife, Maryann, answered. The news wasn't good.

"Kevin's captain called earlier, Gran," Maryann began.

She had been calling her mother-in-law Gran or Granny since she gave birth to Hannah's first grandchild twenty years before. Back then, Hannah and the rest of the family decided the little ones would dub her Granny—as opposed to Grandma or Nana—and soon everyone fell into the habit of calling her that.

"He said Kevin is missing with his company," Maryann continued, "and they are still hopeful of finding them alive."

"That's right, that's right," Hannah said firmly. "We're going to pray everything is all right."

Hannah handed the phone to her husband, Dennis. Maryann repeated the news and Dennis broke down in tears. He gave the phone back to his wife.

Maryann wanted to cry herself. She loved Hannah and Dennis as if they were her own parents. She first met their son in the marching band at St. Joachim's Elementary School. Her brother and Kevin were best friends. And since she married Kevin twenty-one years ago, the two families had grown even closer. She knew it was tearing Hannah and Dennis apart to be away from home. The best thing she could do was to be strong for them. She measured her words and the tone of her voice.

"We're not going to give up hope," Maryann told Hannah.

"That's right," Hannah agreed.

Before hanging up, Hannah once again mistakenly said she was somewhere in Nova Scotia. At a legion hall, she added. She didn't know the phone number.

DAY TWO

Wednesday

September 12

CHAPTER SIX

Courtesy of George Vitale

George Vitale, Appleton mayor Derm Flynn, and Tom McKeon.

Roxanne Loper couldn't sleep. Having all of the families with young children in one room might have seemed like a good idea, but it also meant there wasn't a moment in the entire night when somebody's child wasn't awake and crying. She was naturally restless anyway. She never slept well away from home, and by now she'd been away for more than three weeks. As her husband, Clark, and their newly adopted baby, Alexandria, slept, she found herself wandering the halls of the Lions Club.

Periodically Roxanne would visit the kitchen, where Bruce MacLeod stayed up through the night in case anyone needed anything. Roxanne and MacLeod had hit it off from the start.

"Looks like you're going to be here a while," he'd say.

"Maybe we should start looking for a place," she'd deadpan. "What's a cabin sell for up here?"

Roxanne had noticed a motorcycle parked out front, and when Bruce told her it belonged to him, she knew they were kindred spirits. She used to own a motorcycle back in Texas.

In the morning, more members of the Lions Club showed up to cook the passengers a huge breakfast. Leading the efforts was Stan Nichol, the Lions Club's unofficial culinary master, whose regular job was being the lead cook for the Lakeside Senior Home. Nichol and his crew whipped up a batch of eggs, bacon, sausage, toast, coffee, and fried bologna for the passengers. Being from Texas, Roxanne and Clark had never heard of anyone frying bologna before and found it a little disconcerting when they saw their two-year-old, who was normally a finicky eater, gobbling it down as if it was the best thing she'd ever tasted.

After breakfast, a woman Roxanne and Clark had never seen before asked if she could drive them somewhere in town. For instance, did they need anything from the store? Would they like to go to the Wal-Mart? Roxanne and Clark were both eager. None of the passengers had access to their luggage, since it was all still on the planes. And in the case of Roxanne and Clark, they had been wearing the same clothes for almost three days and thought a change was in order. Especially Clark.

After adopting Alexandria in Kazakhstan, they'd had to fly out through Russia. At the airport in Moscow, Alexandria had thrown up all over Clark, and the only shirt he could find in the airport gift shop was black with www.RUSSIA.RU written across the chest. He didn't mind the writing, but the shirt was about two sizes too small. When he tried it on at the airport he was embarrassed by how skintight it was, but figured he would be home in a few hours and could make the best of it. A few hours was now looking like a few days, and Clark was growing tired of the strange looks he was getting from the other passengers.

"Are you the plane people?" folks inside the store asked, and then wished them well. Some of the locals offered their condolences for what was happening inside the United States. "We're so sorry for you," they'd say mournfully, as if a member of Roxanne and Clark's family had just died.

Roxanne and Clark decided to buy something comfortable to wear, a change of underwear, and some deodorant. No sooner had they returned to the Lions Club than another woman whom they hadn't seen before asked if they would like to take a shower. Roxanne hadn't seen any showering facilities, but assumed they must be tucked away in a part of the club that this woman would now show them.

"No," the woman said. "You can come over to me house and shower."

Roxanne stopped herself from laughing. A complete stranger was inviting her to her home to use the shower. Roxanne and Clark had both grown up in small towns, but this went well beyond small-town hospitality. These were the nicest people in the world, Roxanne thought.

The woman lived only a hundred yards from the Lions Club, so Roxanne, Clark, and Alexandria walked over. Both Roxanne and Clark were amazed at how much better they felt after showering and changing into a clean set of clothes. The woman told them to take as much time as they wanted to relax in the living room before heading back to the Lions Club. The house was quiet. It was the first peaceful moment the couple had in days.

❚

Rose Shepard had lived in Newfoundland for forty-eight years, but when she heard one of the airplanes stranded in Gander was an Aer Lingus jet, the national airline of her beloved Ireland, she knew immediately what she had to do.

"You find out where they are staying," she told her husband, Doug, "and you go there and bring home some nice Irish people for me to talk to."

Rose had been born in Donegal County, west of Belfast, in the far northern reaches of Ireland. During World War II she'd gone to England to train as a nurse, and in 1953 arrived in Newfoundland as part of Britain's overseas nursing service. Three years later she married Doug Shepard, whose family has lived in Newfoundland since the middle of the nineteenth century.

A retired businessman, Doug Shepard was mayor of Gander for sixteen years. Although he hasn't held that title since 1993, some folks still refer to him as Mr. Mayor. Finding the Aer Lingus passengers was easy enough, and when he arrived at the Royal Canadian Legion, he searched out the group's president, Wally Crummell.

"I understand you have some Aer Lingus passengers here," Shepard began, and proceeded to explain his wife's instructions.

A wry little smile crept across Crummell's face, as if he had just solved a great riddle. He led Shepard across the room.

"Here's a nice couple," he offered. "This is Lenny and Maria O'Driscoll."

As much as Crummell liked the wily old Newf, he knew it was probably best for everyone if Lenny and his wife had more private accommodations. Shepard introduced himself and asked the O'Driscolls if they would like to stay at his house with his wife while they were in Gander.

"Oh, that'll be great," Lenny said without hesitation. "Let's go."

▌

George Vitale laced up his running shoes.

Since arriving in Appleton early Wednesday morning, he had tried to keep himself busy and away from the images on television. Running was one of his best outlets. He had been fortunate in this respect, because rather than checking his luggage at the airport in Ireland, he had packed everything in a single garment bag and carried it aboard the plane. As a result, he was one of the few passengers who actually had access to a change of clothes and personal belongings.

Vitale was thrilled to have had a change of clothes and underwear, but it was his running shoes that lifted his spirits. Running had long been a source of comfort for him, a peaceful time away from the stress of his job as a New York State trooper. Each day before work he would set off from his Brooklyn apartment and jog along the waterway separating that borough from Staten Island. The first half of his run would be south, with his back to Manhattan. He ran under the Verrazano Bridge and then turned and proceeded north, the southern tip of Manhattan on the horizon with the towers acting almost like a beacon. Through the first half of the nineties, when the governor's office was located at the World Trade Center, he'd finish his run and then dress and go to work in the South Tower, where he oversaw security in the governor's Manhattan headquarters.

As he started off on his run through the hilly streets of Appleton, he tried to imagine what his jogs would be like when he was home again. He wondered if he would have the strength to run toward a Manhattan skyline missing its towers. Setting a slow and easy pace, he thought about the last two days. On the plane he'd worried most about his best friend from childhood, Anthony DeRubbio, a firefighter in Brooklyn. After initially thinking only about Anthony, Vitale started to wonder about Anthony's older brother, Dominick, who was a battalion chief in the FDNY. While he was still on the plane, Vitale had learned that many of the missing firefighters were among the department's command staff. As a battalion chief, Dominick was probably right there with them. Was he missing? Was he alive or dead? When Vitale first arrived in Appleton and was able to talk to his own family, it was one of the first questions he asked.

"How's Anthony?" Vitale asked his brother, Dennis.

"He's okay," Dennis said without much excitement.

Vitale was elated.

"And Dominick?"

"He's fine," Dennis said. "But David's missing."

David DeRubbio was one of Anthony's younger brothers. He was a firefighter with Engine 226 in downtown Brooklyn and was part of the first wave of firefighters to reach the towers. He was thirty-eight years old and had come to the fire department late in life, deciding to follow in the path of three of his brothers. The fifth of seven children, he'd been on the job only three years. He had a wife and a twelve-year-old daughter.

Vitale felt guilty for having worried only about Anthony and Dominick, and not really thinking about David. He remembered David DeRubbio as a funny kid and a good dad. Strikingly handsome, with blond hair and blue eyes, David was always telling jokes. And he had the type of laugh that would draw people in. In his mind, Vitale could see David Roller-blading through their Brooklyn neighborhood of Bay Ridge or playing roller hockey with his brother Anthony. And he could remember how excited David had been when he learned he'd been accepted to the firefighter training academy. For David, being a firefighter was the missing piece to his life, and besides his wife and daughter, there was nothing he loved more. Except maybe the New York Rangers. He wore a Rangers insignia on his fire helmet. Vitale laughed as he recalled how it befuddled David that his twelve-year-old daughter, Jessica, was a die-hard Islanders fan.

Following the river, which curved its way through Appleton, Vitale wanted to clear his mind for a few minutes while he ran. He turned up the volume on his Walkman and listened to a tape of the soundtrack from the movie *Meet Joe Black*. The Brad Pitt film was basically forgettable, but its music, scored by composer Thomas Newman, was powerful. The cousin of singer, songwriter, and composer Randy Newman, Thomas Newman had scored such films as *American Beauty* and *The Shawshank Redemption*. His work for *Meet Joe Black* featured haunting, emotional, classically inspired orchestral pieces. They were dark, almost funereal in nature, setting the tone for a movie whose main character was a personification of Death.

Although it just happened to be the tape he brought with him to Ireland, it was a fitting backdrop for the moment. The somber notes filled Vitale's ears and stood in stark contrast to the beauty around him—the green canopy of trees, the pale blue sky, the perfectly trimmed and painted homes overlooking the river. Alone and seemingly in the middle of nowhere, he felt useless being so far away from home. He should be in New York, he thought, helping, doing his job, doing something constructive like trying to find David and the others. He felt the road beneath his feet and again tried to clear his mind. All he wanted to do was sweat and let his body take over. The harder he ran, the more distance he temporarily placed between himself and his grief.

After several miles he arrived back at the community center. As always, the television was on, showing news reports and old footage. Local volunteers were on hand, too. Since the community center didn't have shower facilities, Cindy and Reg Wheaton took Vitale to their home just down the street. They told him to help himself to anything in the refrigerator and to use the phone to make calls or the computer to send e-mails. They showed him where the remote for the cable television was located, handed him a clean towel, and left. He could stay as long as he wanted, and they told him that when he was done, he should just leave the door unlocked on the way out. Vitale was speechless when they left. Although the Wheatons thought nothing of leaving a stranger in their home, it was an act of faith Vitale desperately needed at that moment. Something to replace the pain he was feeling. A reassuring sign that the world wasn't as stark as the music that was still echoing in his head.

▌

General Barbara Fast—the intelligence chief for the United States military command overseeing Europe, Africa, and parts of the Middle East—awoke early Wednesday morning after spending the night sleeping on the floor of an American Airlines jumbo jet. Fast had given up her seat for the night to allow a pregnant woman from India to stretch out in the row they had been sharing. The forty-seven-year-old Fast didn't mind sleeping in a cramped, uncomfortable space. After all, she was career military.

She had joined the army in 1976 to take advantage of the GI Bill as a way to pay for graduate school. It didn't take long, however, for her to see a future in the service. From the outset of her career she was assigned to intelligence units, mostly in

Europe. Her undergraduate degree was in German and she was fluent both in that language and in Spanish. She rose steadily through the ranks and was promoted to general in July 2000, while on assignment with the National Security Agency.

In June, she was named director of intelligence for the joint United States European Command, which made her one of the country's key players in the war on terrorism. And yet here she was, trapped on a plane for more than twenty hours. The plane's phone and her cell phone worked only intermittently, but she'd had enough communication with her staff in Stuttgart to know they were doing everything they could to deal with the crisis and to find a way to get her home.

From time to time she wandered to the front of the plane, where the door was open, to survey the scene. She was quite familiar with Gander, because the U.S. military often used it as a refueling stop. She also recalled the Arrow Air plane crash of 1985 and the loss of all those young soldiers from the 101st Airborne. From her vantage point on the plane, Fast could see that the airport was surrounded by trees. She could also see an amazing assortment of commercial airliners.

By midmorning Wednesday, a row of yellow school buses pulled up to her plane and the passengers were allowed off. Striking up a conversation with the bus driver, Fast learned about their strike and how they had all voluntarily come off the picket line when they learned about the diverted flights. Fast was impressed.

Fast could see that security inside the airport was being handled by both the RCMP and a detachment from the Canadian military base. After going through a metal detector, Fast placed her carry-on luggage on a table in front of a young soldier. Although she wasn't wearing a uniform, she was carrying her military identification, and when the soldier spotted it and noticed her rank, he adopted a very formal manner. She noticed that while the passengers before her on line seemed to speed right through, he was taking an exceptionally long time with her. She surmised that the young man, out of a sense of pride, was showing her that he would be thorough and deliberate in accomplishing his task. When he was done, Fast nodded her approval.

There were 154 passengers aboard American Airlines Flight 49, and once they had made their way through the airport, they were taken to the Knights of Columbus hall in the center of town. Even though Fast was off the plane, there was still little she could do but wait. After showering nearby at the community center, she decided to see if she could accomplish a few of the chores her husband had given her to do while she was in the United States. (She called it her "honey-do list." As in: "Honey, do this for me" and "Honey, do that for me.") Although it didn't look like she would make it to the States, she thought she might find a few of the items in Gander.

Most of the items were things her husband had trouble finding in Germany. The big item: a Sears catalog featuring Craftsman tools. As luck would have it, there was a small Sears outlet store—not a full-blown Sears—on the outskirts of town. Fast got directions and set off on foot. She could easily have found a ride with someone if she'd wanted to, but she liked the idea of walking after being confined to a plane for so long.

The walk also gave her more time to think. Earlier, when she arrived at the Knights of Columbus, she saw for the first time, on TV, what had happened. She thought back over all of the bits of intelligence information her command had assembled over the last few months. Was there something they had missed, something they should have seen or detected that would have allowed them to prevent this attack? There were some indications that bin Laden's network had been more active in recent months, Fast thought, but nothing that would have suggested such a brazen assault on the United States.

She refused to allow any doubts to gnaw at her or cause her to feel a sense of guilt. She believed the men and women in her command had done the best they could with the information they had.

Fast found herself on a residential street, where she spotted a man on a porch waving at her. He asked if she was one of the stranded passengers.

"Yes," she said.

He explained that he and his family were preparing a big birthday party for his grandson in the backyard. He asked if she'd like to join them. She agreed and followed him around the house. The boy's parents were still decorating the backyard with balloons and streamers in anticipation of other children arriving. Fast was introduced to the guest of honor.

"Happy birthday," she said.

"Thank you," the boy replied.

"How old are you?"

"Seven," he answered.

Fast was energized by the family's sense of warmth and their willingness to share this time with an outsider who just happened to be walking down the street. For a moment she could almost forget what a dangerous place the world was and the horrors of the preceding day. But she didn't stay long. She didn't need to. A little of that warmth went a long way. Besides, she still wanted to make it to the Sears store before it closed.

▌

While the one-star general explored the town, another passenger from American Airlines Flight 49, Lisa Zale, surveyed the Knights of Columbus building and had her own epiphany. After spending a night on the plane, the thirty-eight-year-old Zale was anxious for a little space. Rather than sleeping each night indoors, crowded together as they had been on the plane, why not camp out on the front lawn? Zale was traveling with her business partner, Sara Wood. They had been to Paris for a trade show and were on their way home to Dallas. "Let's just sleep out here," Zale told Wood, pointing to stretch of green grass between the Knights of Columbus building and the sidewalk.

Wood initially thought Lisa was crazy. Who sleeps on the street when they can be indoors on a cot? Besides, unlike Zale, the forty-five-year-old Wood had never been camping. Zale told her to have a little faith. Following the main road, the two women walked about a half mile to the Wal-Mart. They bought a lantern and a few other items, but the store was out of air mattresses and sleeping bags. So the ladies moved on to Canadian Tire. As its old slogan implies, Canadian Tire is more than just tires. One of the clerks was able to scrounge up a pair of air mattresses and two sleeping bags and then asked, "Do you want a tent as well?"

Zale said it wasn't necessary, but Wood cut her off.

"Hell, yes, we want a tent," she declared, her Texas accent almost bowling the clerk over. It might rain, Wood reasoned, so a tent could come in handy. Zale and Wood piled their supplies onto the checkout counter and started reaching for their credit cards.

"You're off the plane, right?" the cashier asked.

When Zale and Wood nodded, the cashier announced that they could just take the items. Anything the stranded passengers needed, the store was happy to provide. The store even offered to send one of their employees over to the Knights of Columbus to help them set up the tent. The two women were awed by how generous everyone in the store had been.

Zale and Wood loaded their gear into a shopping cart they had taken from Wal-Mart and pushed it back the half mile to the lodge.

∎

Every business in Gander joined the relief effort. The local Kentucky Fried Chicken and Subway sandwich outlets, as well as the local pizza joints, sent carloads of food to the airport on Tuesday and Wednesday to help feed the passengers stranded on the planes. Gander's food co-op, one of the two supermarkets in town, went to twenty-four-hour service in case any of the shelters needed an item from their shelves.

Newtel, the telephone company for Newfoundland, set up a long bank of tables on the sidewalk in front of its offices and filled them with telephones so passengers could make free long-distance phone calls to their families. On another set of outdoor tables, they placed computers with Internet access. Newtel officials kept the tables running day and night for as long as the passengers needed them.

Rogers Communications, which provides cable-television service to Gander and the surrounding area, made sure every shelter had cable television so the passengers could watch CNN and the other round-the-clock news stations. By the time the first busload of passengers was heading for town, technicians for Rogers were already running temporary cable lines into the local churches where they would be staying. Rogers also operates the public-access television station in Gander, Channel 9. The station became a giant bulletin board where messages were posted to help organize relief efforts.

The town's radio station also broadcast dispatches. An urgent plea for toilet paper at St. Paul's brought people running to the school with rolls of tissue from their own homes.

After handling the initial nicotine crisis caused by the smoking ban aboard the plane, Kevin O'Brien, owner of MediPlus Pharmacy, rallied the other pharmacists in the area to face an even more daunting challenge. Many of the passengers had packed their prescription medication away in their luggage before leaving Europe. Since all of their bags were still on the plane, they were desperate to have those prescriptions replaced while they were stranded.

In most cases, the passengers didn't have their actual prescriptions with them. In each case, O'Brien and the other pharmacists had to call the hometown doctor or pharmacist so they would know the exact medication and dosage, and had a new prescription sent. During one stretch, O'Brien and his wife, Rhonda, worked forty-two hours straight, making calls to a dozen different countries.

Surprisingly, there isn't one universal standard for identifying drugs. A drug such as Atenol, commonly prescribed to patients with high blood pressure, can go by different names in different countries. A pharmacist for more than twenty years, O'Brien spent hours on the Internet, and worked with the local hospital and Canadian health officials, to sort through the maze of prescriptions and find the right drugs for each passenger. In the first twenty-four hours, pharmacists in Gander filled more than a thousand prescriptions. All at no cost to the passengers.

For O'Brien, an event like this was the reason he loved living in Gander. A Newfoundlander all his life, he was proud of the way his community would pull together and help one another—or for that matter, a complete stranger. It was a spirit he wanted his three daughters to know and understand, and it was the reason he would never leave.

█

Patricia O'Keefe spent most of the morning trying to find the phone number for the American Legion hall in Nova Scotia. That was all the information she had on the whereabouts of her parents, Hannah and Dennis O'Rourke. Apart from having the wrong Canadian province, she was also obviously asking for the wrong country's legion hall. Later everyone in the family would laugh about it. For now it drove them crazy. Somewhere out there, Hannah and Dennis were stranded with no way of getting home, and their son Kevin was trapped inside one of the fallen towers of the World Trade Center.

Patricia missed having her parents at home, especially her mother. Hannah was the one everyone turned to in a crisis, the person who held things together. She made sure things were done before anyone else thought about them, and would make everything seem effortless in the process. Patricia wanted to try to fill that void. And even though she was married, with children of her own, she still worried about whether she was up to it. Could she offer the type of support to the rest of her family they would need in the days ahead?

█

After catching a couple of hours' sleep, Hannah O'Rourke asked for directions to the Catholic church. The morning sky was clear and a breeze moved through the trees lining the four blocks she walked from the Royal Canadian Legion hall. The church, St. Joseph's, is located in a part of Gander dominated by religious institutions. The Anglican church is close by, as is the United. And farther down the road are the Baptist and the Evangelical.

St. Joseph's is a beautiful new church with a great steeple. When Hannah arrived at the church she was met by Father David Heale, a priest for the last thirty years whose family has lived in Newfoundland for three generations. Father Heale was standing on the front steps, greeting parishioners before morning Mass. Not recognizing Hannah, he quickly guessed she was one of the stranded passengers.

"Good morning," he offered.

Hannah held his hand and tried to remain composed.

"Father, would you pray for our son?" she asked. "He's a firefighter and he's missing in New York."

After morning Mass, Hannah walked back to the legion hall and called her daughter. She felt helpless being so far away.

"We haven't heard anything yet," Patricia told her.

Hannah was quiet.

"Don't give up hope, Ma," Patricia said. "You know Kevin; he'll find a way out. He's a survivor. There are air pockets all over the place."

"I know," Hannah said, not wanting to seem pessimistic.

Finally Patricia asked, "Where are you?"

Between calls to Aer Lingus, the Red Cross, and the Salvation Army, Patricia and her husband, Kevin O'Keefe, had finally pieced together that Hannah and Dennis were in Newfoundland and not Nova Scotia. By now, Hannah had realized it as well. Before she hung up, Hannah gave Patricia the phone number for the legion hall.

Throughout the day, Hannah and Dennis talked to Patricia and Kevin's wife, Maryann, hoping for news. The message, though, was always the same: nothing to report, but don't lose faith.

Now that her family in New York finally knew where Hannah and Dennis were, they attempted to make their own arrangements to bring them home. Maryann's brother offered to drive up and bring them back by car, if necessary. Patricia's husband, Kevin O'Keefe, even tried to reach Senator Hillary Clinton. He talked to a member of Clinton's staff and explained the situation, and the staffer told him she would try to help.

Several of the people from town offered their homes to Hannah and Dennis. But they refused. They were terrified that if they moved out of the legion hall, someone trying to find them might not know where they were. The hard part of being inside the legion was finding ways to avoid watching the news on television. Neither Hannah nor Dennis could bear to watch scenes of the devastation in New York.

Sensing their need for distraction, folks at the legion were taking turns sitting with the anguished couple. Karen Johnson, the wife of the legion's bar manager who was eight months pregnant, visited each day so she could spend time with Hannah. Her pregnancy gave the two women something to talk about, from one mother to another.

And then there was Beulah Cooper. Treasurer of the ladies' auxiliary for the Royal Canadian Legion in Gander, Cooper had been at the hall almost nonstop since September 11. She had three of the passengers staying in her home and had let about a dozen others come over to use her shower.

On Wednesday she convinced Dennis, his nephew Brendan Boyle, and his girlfriend, Amanda, who had been traveling with the older couple, to come to her home, shower, and relax for a couple of hours away from the crowded and noisy hall. Hannah, however, refused to leave. Cooper, a retired government employee, assured her that the folks at the legion would pass along her—Cooper's—number, but Hannah didn't want to take the chance. Except for the two hours each day she spent going to morning and evening Mass, Hannah did not set foot outside the legion hall.

If Hannah wouldn't leave, Cooper decided to try to find other ways to help. She felt a special affinity for Hannah because her son is a volunteer firefighter in Gander. Whenever she hears the sirens of a fire truck, she worries about him. She tried to imagine multiplying that feeling a thousandfold and then having to live with it for days on end.

She knew she couldn't take away the other woman's pain, but she might be able to distract Hannah from it for a few minutes at a time. An unreserved woman, Cooper was boisterous and outgoing. And when it came to telling jokes, Cooper was a Newfie Shecky Greene. She loved giving a joke life, and sitting alongside Hannah, she'd fire away:

> *A fella comes out of a bar after having one too many drinks and he runs into a priest. "Hey," the fella says, "look at your collar, your shirt's on backward."*
>
> *"I'm a father," the priest explains to the man.*
>
> *"So am I," the fella replies.*
>
> *"Yes, but I'm the father to many," the priest offers.*
>
> *"Well, in that case," the fella says, "you should have your pants on backward instead of your shirt."*

When Cooper would finish a joke, Hannah would smile, sometimes even laugh, which only encouraged Cooper to tell more.

CHAPTER SEVEN

Courtesy of Linda Humby

A treat for Ralph.

Excluding the crews, there were officially 6,132 passengers on board the thirty-eight flights, but Bonnie Harris feared there were actually more. Had anybody in authority bothered to check the cargo holes in the belly of the planes? Or were they too overwhelmed to search these jumbo jets thoroughly? All night Tuesday she imagined the worst. She kept picturing hidden travelers lying in the darkness of the planes, desperate to get out, ready to do God knows what.

Bright and early Wednesday morning, she decided to find

out for herself. She didn't trust the people running the operation to know what was really going on, so she called the work area for the ground crews directly.

"Do you have any animals on these planes?"

Just as she suspected, they did. The manifests for twelve of the flights showed the planes were carrying an assortment of animals, including at least nine dogs, ten cats, and a pair of extremely rare Bonobo monkeys. Harris asked if anyone had made arrangements to feed or provide water for any of the animals, who, by this point, had been cooped up in tiny cages aboard the planes for almost twenty-four hours. The answer was no. That was all Harris needed to hear. For five years she'd worked for the local chapter of the Society for the Protection of Cruelty to Animals (SPCA) and was currently the manager of the town's only animal shelter.

"You just can't leave them like that," she complained.

Harris called one of her assistants, Vi Tucker, and the two women loaded up a truck with pet food, water, cleaning supplies, and anything else they thought they might need, and lit out for the airport. Once they arrived, they began sizing up the situation. The animals were stowed away in cages in the same compartments as the luggage. As Harris went around taking a quick look inside each of the planes, she knew these animals were going through their own emotional ordeals. In some cases, Harris couldn't even see the animals, as they were buried behind mounds of suitcases. But she could hear them crying and barking.

At first she tried to convince airport officials to let her and Vi take the animals off of the planes so they could be fed and cared for properly. A representative for Canada's agriculture department, however, refused even to consider it. The official was worried the animals might get loose and introduce some strange disease into the country. Rather than go to war with the bureaucrat, Harris and Tucker and another SPCA worker, Linda Humby, decided to make the best of the situation.

One at a time they crawled into the belly of the airplanes, tunneling their way through the mountains of bags, to reach each animal. As best they could, they would clean the cage and then lay out some food and water.

In addition to being cramped, it was also hot. And it smelled. The worst part, though, was seeing the animals, who were obviously scared and disoriented. The women looked for tags on each of the cages that might give the animal's name, so that the animal might hear something reassuring. Since they were all coming over from Europe, the woman thought, these pets might not understand a lot of English, but every dog and cat can recognize its name.

On a British Airways plane, they found a cat that had a pill taped to the front of its cage. The cat was apparently epileptic and needed regular medication to ward off seizures. Aboard a Lufthansa flight were two Siamese cats and a ten-week-old purebred American cocker spaniel with the name tag RALPH pinned to the door. The women fell in love with Ralph immediately.

As the woman went from one plane to the next, they became increasingly frustrated. It would take them more than ten hours to visit the twelve planes the animals were on. By the time they finished, they were covered in sweat, dirt, and an assortment of other stains they didn't even want to think about.

"This isn't going to work," Harris told Humby. "It took us all day to feed them just one meal."

Some of the animals—such as the epileptic cat—would need medication on a regular basis. The only good news was that they didn't have to worry about the monkeys. The Bonobos were on their way from Belgium to a zoo in Ohio and were being tended to by their handler. Nevertheless, the women were going to need more help with the dogs and cats. Most of all, they needed to get those animals off the plane. Desperate, they called the government's regional veterinarian, Doug Tweedie.

Doc Tweedie was stunned when Harris told him what was happening. On Tuesday, he had been forty miles away in Bishop Falls tending to a sick cow when he heard about the terrorist attack in the United States and learned of the diverted flights to Gander. Suspecting there might be animals on some of the planes, he asked his wife to check into it. When she called Gander's town hall on Tuesday, she was told there were no animals on any of the flights—a message she passed on to her husband.

Now he suddenly learned there were animals on those planes. And after hearing the horror stories from Harris, Tweedie leaped into action. After several phone calls to his superiors in St. John's, a deal was reached whereby the animals could be taken off the plane and kept in a vacant hangar where the women could care for them.

"Thank God," Humby said when she heard the news from Doc Tweedie. She knew if they hadn't received permission to remove the animals, some of them would have certainly died.

▌

As the heroines of the SPCA continued their mission of mercy, Constable Oz Fudge was busy honoring a long-distance request from a fellow police officer. Earlier in the day he received a phone call from Sheryl McCollum, an investigator with the Cobb County Police Department in Marietta, Georgia.

"I have a favor to ask," McCollum began.

"I'm cheap and I'm easy and I'll do whatever you want," Fudge replied.

"My sister Sharlene Bowen is on one of the flights," McCollum explained. "She's a flight attendant with Delta. She's staying at the Irving West, room 214. I want you to go down there and give her a hug and tell her that we miss her and we can't wait for her to come home."

"All right," Fudge said.

"Now, you remember that a promise is a promise," McCollum said.

"Yes, my dear," Fudge said. "Don't worry about a thing. I promise."

Fudge drove to the hotel, but the forty-five-year-old Bowen wasn't there. He left her a note, cryptically saying he had a message for her. He also left her a present, a Gander Police Department patch.

While Fudge was visiting the hotel, Bowen was walking around town. A flight attendant on Delta Flight 15, Bowen was the middle child in a family of five sisters. All of the sisters were extremely close; none of them had heard from Bowen since her plane was diverted to Gander.

Bowen had managed only a brief phone call to her husband, using the cell phone of one of the passengers. When she first arrived at the hotel from the plane, she tried again, but all of the circuits were busy. Rather than sit in the room and wait for the phones to work, Bowen decided to take a look around. And after thirty hours on the plane she needed to stretch her legs and get a little fresh air.

Back in Georgia, McCollum wasn't willing to wait. Using her detective skills, she had tracked down her sister's where-abouts and then called Fudge.

An hour or so after Fudge departed, Bowen returned to the hotel and discovered the note and the patch waiting for her at the front desk, and assumed they must have been some sort of a message for the crew from Delta. The town's municipal building was only a couple of blocks away, and thinking the police department might be housed inside, Bowen, along with the plane's pilot and several of her fellow crew members, walked over.

Fudge wasn't there, but the group did run into Mayor Claude Elliott. The mayor explained that Fudge was working a security detail at the airport and would contact Bowen later. In the meantime, Elliott asked if the Delta crew would like a tour of his town. They all accepted and then piled into the mayor's car. He drove them to Lake Gander and then out to the airport to see the planes. It was the first time Bowen had a good look at all of the aircraft that had been diverted to Gander.

The mayor then took them over to the community center. Bowen couldn't believe the amount of supplies people were donating. The mayor was extremely proud of his town's efforts. He even took them to the local brewery, where they were given free samples of beer. As the mayor continued his guided tour, his cell phone rang.

"Okay," he said, "I'll swing by my house and pick up my clubs. See you soon."

It was the manager of the local golf course, Elliott explained. They were allowing passengers to play for free, but the course didn't have enough spare sets of clubs to outfit everyone. The course manager was calling his regular customers, hoping they would bring their clubs to the course for the passengers to borrow. So far everybody the manager contacted had said yes.

By the time Bowen returned to the hotel several hours later, she found another note from Fudge and a police department baseball cap. This time, though, Fudge had left his phone number.

"Don't move," he implored when she called. "I'll be there in five minutes."

Three minutes later Fudge arrived. Bowen was standing in the lobby, still not sure why he needed to talk to her. The constable walked up to her and, without saying anything, wrapped his arms around her and squeezed tight.

"That's from your sister," he finally said.

CHAPTER EIGHT

George, Deb, Lana, Bill, Edna, and Winnie reunite in Houston, April 16, 2002.

Twenty-four hours after the attack on the World Trade Center, there were still passengers on board a handful of planes in Gander waiting to be processed. Despite the delay, the 116 people aboard Continental Flight 5 from London to Houston were in amazingly good spirits. This was largely attributable to three factors. First, everyone recognized that in light of the tragic events in the United States, they had no right to complain. Second, they understood that griping wouldn't do any good anyway, so they might as well make the best of it. And third, the flight attendants had unlocked the liquor carts and were letting everyone pour their own drinks for free.

Once the sun went down on Tuesday, the plane developed the vibe of a freewheeling United Nations cocktail party, with passengers mixing, mingling, and imbibing. It was during this revelry that Deborah Farrar sipped her first gin-and-tonic. Her trip overseas had been full of firsts for the twenty-eight-year-old Texan—the most significant being that it was the first time she'd ever been outside the United States. The whole point of this vacation was to take chances, experience new things, and expand her horizons; and although the reason for her current predicament was tragic, she found herself enjoying the company of the other passengers.

Ten days earlier she'd taken off from her job as an account executive for an information technology firm in Houston and had flown off to Europe all by herself. She went to Oslo and Bergen in Norway for the first six days before ending up in London. She was due back at work later in the week but now found herself in a place she had never heard of before and in the midst of something she wasn't quite sure how to handle.

When the plane landed Tuesday afternoon and the pilot announced what happened in New York, Farrar broke down in tears. She wanted to talk to her family, hear their voices, and let them know she was okay, but none of the phones on the plane had worked. Eventually, a cell phone belonging to one of the passengers in first class locked onto a usable signal, and the man let everyone on board make a call. A line stretched down the aisle of the aircraft as one by one his fellow passengers and the flight's crew members talked to loved ones back home for a few minutes. Five hours after landing, Farrar reached her father.

Being able to call home had had a liberating effect on most of the passengers, and the tension on the plane lifted. Rather than worrying about family members who might be worried about them, they mainly concentrated on piercing the boredom of being trapped on a plane all night. Also, no one on board seemed to have a direct connection to the tragedy—no family members in New York or Washington who might be missing or dead. Their only real link was the bits of news they would receive.

Inside the cockpit, the pilot's radio was tuned to a news station broadcasting nonstop reports from the United States. From time to time passengers would poke their heads in to listen. Whether the pilot realized it or not, leaving the cockpit door open proved to be incredibly reassuring for those on board. Rather than feeling alone and isolated, they knew they had access to the latest news without having it forced on them. It was up to each passenger to decide how immersed in the details of the day's events he or she wanted to be.

Once the flight attendants served the last of the food, they rolled out the carts containing those marvelous miniature bottles of booze. The attendants set them up by the back of the plane and then walked away. A few passengers promptly donned aprons and played bartender. So while those interested in listening to news reports huddled near the cockpit, those who wanted to escape flocked to the rear of the aircraft.

The mood was set by a group of wealthy oilmen from first class. One in particular, Bill Cash, was feeling especially social. Cash owns a company that helps build offshore oil platforms. He had been born in England but married a girl from Alabama, and they now lived in Houston. At fifty-one, Cash was the kind of fellow who could start a party just by walking into a room. As far as he was concerned, a stranded jumbo jet was as good a place as any for a good time.

It didn't take long for him and Deb to become friends. She proved to be just as outgoing as he was. Her gin and tonic was the idea of one of Cash's fellow businessmen and it sounded good to her. When one of the flight attendants heard it was the first time Deb had ever had this particular libation, she raced off to the galley. Returning a few moments later, she plopped a wedge of lime in Deb's drink.

"You can't have your very first gin and tonic without lime," the flight attendant said. "It wouldn't be right."

Farrar was awestruck by the different people she met. Two of the women she befriended on the plane were Lana Etherington and Winnie House. The first thing Deb noticed about Winnie was how strikingly beautiful the twenty-six-year-old was. Winnie was tall and slender, like a model. And her hair, tied in braids, stretched all the way down to the small of her back. Born in Asaba, Nigeria, where her father is a village chieftain, Winnie spent a lot of her time growing up in London. Fluent in both English and her native language of Igbo, she also spoke a little French. She attended college in Oklahoma and had recently settled in Houston. On September 11, she was flying home to Houston after visiting her sister in London.

Lana was also from Africa. She had grow up in what was then known as Rhodesia and received a law degree from the University of Rhodesia. She left the former British colony in 1980 as the white-controlled government was being replaced by Robert Mugabe, a guerrilla-leader-turned-dictator who renamed the nation Zimbabwe. From Africa, Lana moved to the Middle East, where she worked for Pan American Airways as an executive secretary. While living in Dubai for five years, she married an American who worked for an oil company. Together for nineteen years, the couple now lives in Houston with their two children. The Lone Star State hasn't made much of a linguistic impression on Lana. She continues to speak with a proper British accent.

Deb, Winnie, and Lana made an eclectic trio: an innocent Texas Aggie, a Nigerian princess, and a globe-trotting mom.

By the time Wednesday morning rolled around, the plane

had been wrung dry of alcohol and most of the passengers had managed only a couple of hours' sleep. Continental Flight 5 was the thirty-fifth plane to be emptied. Bleary-eyed, Deb and her new friends climbed onto yellow school buses for the ride to the terminal building, where they would be taken through Canadian customs and then passed along to the Red Cross for processing. Twenty-nine and a half hours had passed from the time they boarded in London to the time they finally stepped off the plane in Gander.

Most of the shelters in town were already filled when Flight 5 was ready to leave the airport, so they were sent thirty miles down the Trans-Canada Highway to Gambo, a town of 2,300 people located at the confluence of the Gander River and Freshwater Bay. This is the southern edge of Newfoundland's scenic Kittiwake coast, a series of small fishing villages, inlets, and islands that jut into the North Atlantic. The Kittiwake coast stretches from Laurenceton up to Twillingate and Fogo Island, and then down to Port Blanchard. In the late spring and early summer, when the polar ice cap begins to break apart, visitors come to the area to watch the massive icebergs flow into the Atlantic.

For nearly a century, from the 1860s until the 1950s, Gambo was the hub of the area's logging operations. The daily harvest of spruce, fir, and pine trees would be floated down the river to the sawmills in Gambo, where they were cut and then loaded onto railcars. The Great Fire of '61 changed all that. Tens of thousands of acres went up in flames, and with it the economy of Gambo. All that's left is an empty train trestle, a reminder of the town's storied past.

As they drove along the winding roads leading into Gambo, Lana was reminded of the hills and valleys of northern England. It was all so quaint and rural. They arrived at the Salvation Army church early Wednesday afternoon. It seemed as if the whole town had come to welcome them. There was a big pot of beef stew and sandwiches waiting on one table. At another, there were seven women all in line, serving freshly brewed tea in little teacups.

Inside, a television was on, but Deb, Lana, and Winnie ignored it, opting instead to use the phones in the church to call their families. When Lana finished talking to her husband, she noticed that one of her fellow passengers, Mark Cohen, had gone outside to have a cigarette. A closet smoker who hides her habit from her children, Lana joined him. Whether it was conscious or not, Lana made the decision not to see the devastation on television. The fresh air and warm sun on her face had invigorated her. After she'd spent almost thirty hours cooped up on planes and buses, the last thing she wanted to do was to sit indoors and watch the news. She suggested to Mark that they find Deb and Winnie and explore the town a bit. He agreed, and the four of them were soon on their way.

Their plan was simple: find Gambo's one pub. Walking down the road, they made quite a sight. After a few minutes a red van, driven by a man who appeared to be in his early sixties, pulled up alongside them.

"Are you the plane people?" asked the driver, George Neal.

The group nodded, not quite sure what to make of him.

"Do you want to come around for coffee?" he suggested. "I live just down the road. I can give you a lift."

The foursome looked at one another and through a series of discreet nonverbal gestures—a raised eyebrow, a few tiny head shakes, and an assortment of grimaces—quickly came to the conclusion that it probably wasn't a good idea to get into a complete stranger's van. Politely begging off, they told George they were fine and wanted to walk. George said he understood, but if they changed their minds, or if they ever needed a ride somewhere, to just stop by his house. He pointed out where he lived and drove off.

Standing by the road, they all laughed. After all, there must be at least a dozen horror movies that start off with just this type of scenario—a group of friends, out in the middle of nowhere, who hitchhike a ride from a kindly old man and end up struggling for their lives. After walking a few more minutes, they spotted the town store. They pooled their cash—no credit cards accepted—and bought ice cream and potato chips and bottled water. They asked the clerk how far it was to the pub. The answer shocked them. It was still a good two miles away. Gambo may not have had many people in it, but it is long and narrow and winds with the river. The church where the passengers had been dropped off was on the western edge of town, and the pub was on the eastern side. The sun that had felt so good a short time before was now feeling a bit oppressive. None of them wanted to hike another two miles in eighty-degree weather, but they refused to give up on their quest for the next round of cocktails. It was clear what they had to do.

Following the van driver's directions, they approached a large house with off-white vinyl siding and white trim. Mark joked that he would protect them if there was any trouble, and the women laughed nervously. They noticed an older woman standing in the driveway.

"George invited us over for coffee," Deb said.

"You must be the plane people," the woman replied, introducing herself as George's wife, Edna. "Come on in, my dears."

George was inside and was thrilled to see them. As he and Edna scurried off to the kitchen, Deb, Lana, Winnie, and Mark found themselves staring at the couple's big-screen television. It was late Wednesday afternoon, and for the first time they all saw the images of destruction in New York. Until now they had done a good job of distancing themselves from the terror, but as soon as they saw news reports and those pictures, the reality of the last twenty-four hours hit them, hit them in such a way that they could no longer ignore it. Shocked. Shaken. Horrified. There were no words to describe what they were feeling. Deb broke down in tears in the living room. Winnie ran into the bathroom to cry. The others just stood there speechless.

For now at least, the party was over.

CHAPTER NINE

Eithne Smith, Rabbi Leivi Sudak, and Lakewood
Academy principal Jamey Jennings.

Eithne Smith was working the fax machine. Since some
passengers were having trouble reaching loved ones by phone,
many had resorted to sending messages by fax. Inside the
office of the Lakewood Academy, the only school in Glenwood,
Smith was assembling the dispatches from passengers and
feeding them into the machine. She sent so many faxes on
Wednesday that her index finger was starting to swell from her
pounding on the keys.

A native of Newfoundland and a teacher for twenty years,

Smith loved the sense of family evoked in a school the size of Lakewood, with its 220 students and a faculty of seventeen. The school teaches the children of Glenwood and Appleton from kindergarten through grade twelve, and Smith constituted 100 percent of the school's senior history department, 100 percent of the French department, and one-third of the English department. Like all of the teachers, she was used to doing a little bit of everything.

As she continued sending faxes and waiting patiently for confirmation that each had been received, one of the passengers walked into the office. Four planeloads of strandees—more than 650 people—had been sent to Glenwood and the neighboring town of Appleton. The majority of them were staying at the school.

"I've watched you all morning solve other people's problems," the woman said, "and now I have one for you."

The woman explained that there was an Orthodox rabbi in the school, along with at least two women who were Orthodox Jews, and they hadn't eaten since their plane had arrived in Gander more than twenty-four hours earlier because none of the food being served was kosher. They were hungry, but they didn't want to complain to anyone. The woman said she only discovered this when she noticed the people weren't eating and asked them why.

Smith was more than ready for the challenge. Her given name, Eithne, is an ancient Gaelic name that her mother had always loved. The two most recent uses of the name that Smith had found were for an old Irish battleship and a Catholic nun. Her husband often joked that he wasn't sure which of the two she reminded him of more.

In the days following September 11, she was a little bit of both.

Smith promised the woman she'd fix the problem at once, called the main school district office, and told them she needed help. Within an hour the owner of the company that provides meals to the regular flights in and out of Gander drove to Glenwood with a cartonful of kosher meals for the school to use over the next few days.

"How did you know we were hungry?" asked Rabbi Leivi Sudak, when she came to tell them the food had arrived.

Smith told him another passenger had noticed.

"Thank you," he said. "Thank you for everything."

Smith wished they had thought of asking for kosher meals without being prompted. The truth is, there just aren't a lot of Jewish people in Newfoundland. The island is 98 percent Catholic and Protestant, and the only synagogue in the province is more than two hundred miles away in St. John's. As far as she knew, the only Jewish person in Gander was David Zelcer, a correspondent for the CBC.

To help them take care of their needs for the duration of the crisis, the school gave Rabbi Sudak free rein in the faculty lounge, which had a stove, a sink, and a refrigerator. Along with several other Orthodox passengers, the rabbi turned the lounge into a kosher kitchen, complete with new pots, pans, cutlery, and cooking utensils.

Smith felt a great deal of warmth toward Rabbi Sudak, and as she often does to people she likes, she attempted to give him a reassuring hug. When the rabbi realized she was about to touch him, he gently stepped back and folded his arms across his body. He told her he appreciated the gesture, but in his faith it was improper for him to touch a woman.

There were so many different cultures represented in the school, it was just staggering to Smith. Soon after the passengers arrived, school officials hung a large map of the world on the wall and asked everyone to place a thumbtack next to the place they were from. By her count, at Lakewood Academy alone there were people from forty different countries, from Sri Lanka to Tasmania. There were women in burkas and men in flowing robes. The hallways were filled with the sounds of different languages.

After resolving the food crisis, Smith went back to faxing. Before long she was interrupted by a phone call from Australia. The woman on the line was trying to reach her son, Peter. The Red Cross said he had been sent to Glenwood, but Smith couldn't find a record of him on their sheets. The woman was distraught. She had argued with her son before his flight took off and was upset that their last words to each other were filled with anger. Ever since the attacks on the United States, she had been frantically trying to find out where he was to make sure he was safe.

Smith set out to look for the young man. When she was unable to find him, she left notes around the school and on bulletin boards asking him to report to the office as soon as possible. An hour or so later he arrived.

He was a big fellow, tall and blond. He looked like the classic Aussie surfer. Spotting him holding one of the notes she had posted, Smith walked over and gave him a kiss on the cheek. "That's from your mother," she said. "She wants you to call her. She says she's not angry."

Peter started sobbing uncontrollably. "I was afraid to call her," he said. "I thought she would still be mad." Smith took him by the hand and led him into the principal's office and told him to call his mother that very instant.

∎

General Barbara Fast finished her shopping and made it back to the Knights of Columbus building in time for dinner. The volunteers at the fraternal organization had made a point of cooking something special for the passengers on their first night with them and had prepared a roast-beef banquet.

Rather than serving the meal buffet style, the volunteers insisted on each of the 154 passengers taking their seats and being waited on as if they were in a restaurant.

By now, some of the passengers knew what Fast did for a living. Some turned to her for answers. How could something like this have happened? Fast didn't know what to tell them. How do you provide a rational explanation for such an irrational act?

Fast continued receiving updates from her staff in Germany. Initial reports from the Pentagon placed the death toll in the building as being very high, possibly as many as 900. She had walked those halls on many an occasion, and now they were nothing more than smoldering rubble. Ultimately, it was determined that 125 people were killed inside the Pentagon, with another 64 lost on the American Airlines flight that crashed into it.

And when the final lists were released, she counted several friends among those who died, including Lieutenant General Timothy Maude, the army's deputy chief of staff for personnel and the highest-ranking officer killed on September 11. Fast had known General Maude and his family since 1996. The last time they had seen each other, she'd played a round of golf with him and his wife in Germany.

Wednesday was the Knights' regular bingo night, but they canceled the event because of the arrival of their unexpected guests. Fast thought this was a mistake, as the organization could probably have made a fortune selling bingo cards to the passengers, who would have been thrilled by the diversion. Nevertheless, Fast wouldn't have had time to play. After dinner, she spotted several Canadian military officials who were walking straight toward her.

"General Fast," the lead officer said, "I'm Lieutenant Colonel McKeage."

McKeage is the wing commander for the Canadian air

force base in Gander. He apologized for not realizing sooner that she was there. He told her they were going to move her to a secure site on the base where she could speak candidly to her staff and that preparations were being made to get her out of Gander as soon as possible. A great deal had already been happening. While she was in Gander, German police had raided an apartment in Hamburg, where they believed much of the planning for September 11 took place.

In the morning, special arrangements were made to secretly fly Fast to Europe. By Friday, she was back at her command in Stuttgart, where her staff continued to help piece together the circumstances that led up to the attack and hunt for those responsible. Before leaving the Knights of Columbus, she said good-bye to some of the passengers and thanked the volunteers for their kindness.

Driving to the air force base, Fast commented to McKeage how wonderful everyone in town had been. It made her feel part of a family.

"We're all Americans tonight," replied McKeage.

▌

The pilot of Lufthansa Flight 438 stopped by the Lions Club with news. Gathering all of the passengers together in one room, he announced that as soon as the plane was able to take off, they would probably have to return to Frankfurt rather than continuing on to Dallas. No final decision had been made, he added, but flying back to Europe was the most likely scenario.

Roxanne Loper had no intention of going to Germany. She was afraid she would run into immigration problems there with her newly adopted daughter, Alexandria, and that it might take her and Clark weeks to get another flight to the United

States. She wanted to go home, and being in Canada was a lot closer to home than being in Germany.

"Why," Roxanne said, interrupting the pilot, "do we have to go back to Germany? I don't want to go back." The other passengers started voicing their own objections.

The pilot was clearly frustrated by the brewing revolt. By a show of hands, he asked, how many people wanted to go on to the United States? Nearly every hand in the room went into the air.

"Okay," he said, "let me talk to the Lufthansa people."

The uncertainty upset Roxanne. She was adamant about not getting onto a plane that was headed to Germany. "I don't care if I have to ride a camel naked across the border to prove I'm not hiding anything," she told Stan Nichol, the Lions Club chef. "I'd rather do that than fly to Frankfurt and wait for another plane."

Bruce MacLeod could see the strain on Roxanne. She hadn't slept. And she was depressed and embarrassed that Alexandria was still throwing a fit whenever she tried to hold her. Roxanne reminded MacLeod of one of his kids. She was the same age as his daughter, and it hurt him to see Roxanne in such pain. He decided she needed a little break from everyone, and he remembered their conversation the night before about his motorcycle.

"I'm making a run," he told her. "Do you want to come along?"

"You bet," she said, her eyes lighting up.

Roxanne nearly bowled him over heading for the door. MacLeod owns a gold-colored Suzuki Cavalcade, a large bike designed for long-distance travel. It features a 1400 cc engine and all the creature comforts of an automobile—cruise control, AM-FM cassette radio, which could be plugged into their helmets, built-in rear saddlebags for storage. It was more than eight feet long and weighed about nine hundred pounds. Since buying the motorcycle in 1996, MacLeod and his wife, Sue, had traveled throughout Canada on it.

He tossed Roxanne his wife's helmet and sunglasses and she climbed on behind him. The cold evening air felt good. He gave her a tour of the town and took her out to Cobbs Pond, and then they swung by the community center. Roxanne was stunned to see all of the items people were donating and the effort by the town's volunteers to keep everything organized. And she laughed when she saw they were using the town's ice rink to keep perishables from spoiling.

MacLeod was eager to ride out to the airport to see what was happening. As an air-traffic controller, he understood better than most just how historic the events of the last twenty-four hours had been. And like a kid, he wanted to see all of the planes.

The main road leading to the airport was blocked and guarded by Mounties. Fortunately, the guards were local boys and MacLeod asked if it was all right for them to just take a quick look at the airfield.

"She just wants to make sure her plane is still there," he said with a smile.

The Mounties waved them through. MacLeod and Roxanne drove along the airport's perimeter road and stopped near the fence at one end of the runway. The night before, when she stepped off the plane, Roxanne hadn't noticed just how many planes were on the ground. Now that they were all empty, they were parked nose to tail, one after another.

"Wow," she said, getting off the motorcycle. "That is amazing. All those planes. So many people."

Roxanne looked away from MacLeod and stared at the stars in the sky. How could somebody do something so evil, something that adversely affected so many innocent lives? How could somebody have so much hatred for America? She could feel the tears on her face. It was all finally catching up to her: the notion that her country was under attack; the magnitude of the suffering of the families of the dead and missing; the ambiguity over how long she and the others would stay in Gander and where they would go next; the lack of sleep; the lack of privacy; the separation from Samantha; the rejection by Alexandria. On the side of the dark and empty road, dwarfed by the jumbo jets all around her, she allowed herself to cry. Normally she would have been embarrassed to be break down in front of a relative stranger. Yet somehow she felt safe with MacLeod. He was very paternal and protective. When she was done, she climbed back onto the motorcycle and they left. MacLeod took the long way to the club. He'd give her a chance to compose herself.

∎

It was Wednesday night at the Lions Club and Lisa Cox was bored. Apart from watching the nonstop news coverage on television, there wasn't a lot for the eighteen-year-old to do at night. Bruce MacLeod and Stan Nichol joked with her that once her mom went to bed, they would take her and her sister out barhopping around town. Lisa would brighten up and say, "Really." And they would laugh and say, "Maybe." But they were only teasing her, and so at night she just paced around the hall. She spent a lot of time helping parents care for the some of the babies and young children at the Lions Club, a particularly poignant sight given everything Lisa had been through in the last two years with her cancer and the sad reality that she'd never be able to have children of her own.

Hans Larson, the president of the Lions Club, could see she was feeling a bit antsy. A big, lovable walrus of a man, Larson handed her the keys to his van and told her she could go out to the parking lot and listen to music. She was thrilled to be able to be by herself for a little while. Larson's taste in music veered toward country, which wasn't Lisa's favorite, but she did find some old Eric Clapton tapes. She cranked up Larson's stereo, closed her eyes, and imagined herself back home—even if it was just for an hour or so.

▌

Hannah and Dennis O'Rourke returned to St. Joseph's Wednesday night for evening Mass, and Father Heale made a special point of mentioning their plight.

"There is a couple here who are missing a son," he announced, "and I ask you to remember them particularly in your prayers."

In the back of the church, Tom Mercer craned his neck to see who Father Heale was talking about. Mercer was from Port Albert, a town of about eighty-five people on the northeast coast of Newfoundland. On September 11, he'd driven eighty miles from his home to offer himself as a volunteer in Gander. Mostly he had been providing rides around town to any of the passengers who needed one. In two days he had taken dozens of passengers to the mall. He gave a few a sightseeing tour of the area. And then, earlier that night, a group of women from Spain who were staying at Gander Collegiate, wanted to attend evening Mass. Mercer piled them into his car—a brand-new Pontiac—and delivered them to St. Joseph's.

The sixty-five-year-old Mercer isn't Catholic—he's Protestant—but he decided to stay for the service so he could give the women a ride back to their shelter. After Mass, as is customary, everyone went next door to a meeting room where coffee and tea were served. Mercer felt drawn to the

O'Rourkes. He went over to them and told them how sorry he was to hear about their son and that he'd keep them in his thoughts and prayers.

Mercer was struck by what good and decent people the O'Rourkes appeared to be. They were all the same age, so he naturally tried to imagine how he would hold up if it had been his son who was missing.

CHAPTER TEN

Lisa Zale and Sara Wood outside the Knights of Columbus.

Continental Flight 5 passengers Deb Farrar, Winnie House, Lana Etherington, and Mark Cohen had been at George and Edna Neal's home in Gambo for a couple of hours watching the news reports from the United States when the couple excused themselves from the group. George had been sizing up his guests, trying to get a sense of what kind of people they were, and came to the conclusion that he liked them. He asked Edna her impression. She liked them, too. They seemed like a nice mix of young people, she said.

Courtesy of Sara Wood

"Why don't we ask them to stay?" George suggested.

Edna thought it a splendid idea.

George didn't have to wait long for an answer. Given the choice between sleeping in the floor of the church or staying in the Neals' comfortable home, they decided on the comfortable home. Lana couldn't help but think to herself that there wasn't another place like this on earth. Where else would a couple invite four outsiders into their home for the night?

To celebrate their newfound friendships, they decided to go out to dinner. Choosing a place to eat wasn't hard. There's only one restaurant in Gambo: Sheila's. George knew it well. He used to own it. Under his care it was called, matter-of-factly, Roadside Restaurant. In 1981, he sold it to Sheila.

The menu is typical Newfoundland cuisine, which is to say it mostly involves cod. Baked cod. Broiled cod. Deep-fried cod. Panfried cod. Everyone was glad to get out of the house, glad to be away from the television.

In addition to Continental Flight 5, passengers from five other planes had been brought to Gambo. All told, nearly 900 "plane people" found themselves in this remote hamlet. The Society of United Fishermen opened their social hall to accommodate about a hundred passengers. The United Church took in 75, the Anglican Church 140, and the Catholics hosted an even hundred. Down at the volunteer fire department, the fire trucks were moved outside the station so cots could be set up in the engine bays to accommodate 120 people. Others were moved to the Smallwood Academy, the town's only school, which educated Gambo's children from kindergarten right on through the twelfth grade.

From house to house, people stripped their closets of extra bedding, blankets, and pillows and carried them to various shelters. When word spread that the passengers didn't have access to their luggage and had been wearing the same outfits for nearly two days, piles of old—and in some cases new—

clothes magically started appearing. In the neighboring small towns of Glovertown and Dover and Hare Bay, the women decided to pitch in by cooking meals, which were delivered each day to Gambo by a caravan of cars.

Any passenger wanting to take a shower needed only to tap one of the locals on the shoulder to ask. Often they didn't even needed to do this, as people would just walk into one of the shelters and ask aloud: "Who'd like a shower?" Anyone who raised his hand was invited home. Most passengers, however, were still getting their bearings Wednesday evening and remained close to their respective shelters. As a result, George, Edna, Deb, Lana, Winnie, and Mark had no trouble finding a table at the restaurant. The one familiar face they did see belonged to Bill Cash, the animated Texas millionaire from first class. They couldn't help but tease Bill about the good fortune they'd had running into George and Edna and the comfy confines they would now be enjoying.

By the time dinner was completed, they noticed Bill had moved from his table and sidled up to George. Hoping to wrangle an invitation to the house as well, Bill employed all his charm and social skills. He was eager to avoid sleeping on a cot at the firehouse. He had even toyed with the idea of buying one of the houses in Gambo—they were only a few thousand dollars—but they were unfurnished. Before long, George was checking with the others to see if it was okay for Bill to join them. How could they refuse? Especially once Bill agreed to buy all the drinks at the pub that night.

They piled into George's red van and off they went. Around 8 P.M. they finally reached the promised land, the Holy Grail of the day's excursion: Gambo's Trailways Pub. A simple wooden building on a dirt lot, the pub looked a little seedy from the outside. Winnie didn't say anything, but it reminded her of the kind of bars they have on the outskirts of Houston, bars a black person would never go into.

Winnie couldn't help but notice that she was the only black person in town.

The pub was undergoing renovations the week of September 11, but decided to open up anyway in honor of the stranded passengers. There was a temporary bartop set up along one wall, the ceiling was half torn down, and the stage was still under construction.

Regardless of the state the place was in, the pub wasn't about to close its doors during a civic emergency. For the duration of the plane people's stay, the pub would be open damn near twenty-four hours a day, closing only long enough to hose the place down and give the bar staff a chance to sleep.

The pub was jumping with people when George and his newfound friends arrived. Bill gave his credit card to the bartender and told him to start a tab for the group. The jukebox was playing a mix of rock, country, and Newfoundland's own brand of music from groups such as Great Big Sea, the Ennis Sisters, and Buddy Wassisname. Everyone in the group was feeling good again. Since the only one among them who was single was Deb, the others decided to play matchmaker and find her a man.

"We've got to hook you up with somebody." Winnie laughed.

One of the oilmen from first class made a run at Deb, but she brushed him off. He was a little too sure of himself. Not her type.

Finally she spotted somebody. He was about six feet tall. Looked to be in his early thirties. He was fit, without being too muscular. Good-looking but not a pretty boy.

"See that guy over there," she whispered conspiratorially to Lana and Winnie. "Don't you think he looks cute?"

"Oh yeah," Lana said. Winnie agreed.

"How are we going to get him over here?" Lana asked.

Before Deb could think of an answer, Winnie was on her feet.

"Watch this," she told the others. Pointing to the guy across the room, she shouted, "Hey, you, come here!"

Waving one hand over her head as if she were twirling a lasso, Winnie tossed her imaginary rope in the guy's direction and pretended to pull him in. Not needing much more encouragement, the man walked over to the table. Winnie moved an empty chair between her and Deb and told him to have a seat.

"I'd like to introduce you to Deborah," Winnie said.

Deb was blushing, but she didn't mind.

His name was Gregory Curtis, a thirty-one-year-old first lieutenant in the United States Marines. He'd been on his way home to North Carolina following a six-month deployment in Bosnia when his flight was diverted.

∎

Outside the Knights of Columbus building, Lisa Zale and Sara Wood were creating quite a stir with their tent. With the help of one of the other passengers, they set up the green-and-white nylon abode on the front lawn, covered the floor of the tent with the two air mattresses, and placed a pair of sleeping bags inside. To block out the noise from the traffic on the street, they donned the Boze headphones they'd taken with them from their seats in first class. And next to their tent they parked their Wal-Mart shopping cart.

Some of their fellow passengers thought they were crazy until they went to bed that night. Just as Zale had predicted, the accommodations inside the Knights of Columbus building were cramped and noisy. There was a cacophony of snores that kept some passengers awake, and by midnight, Zale and Wood noticed some of the passengers whining to one another in the parking lot: Why didn't we get tents and air mattresses?

∎

Over in Glennwood, a speck of a town east of Gander and just across the river from Appleton, Janet Shaw volunteered for the graveyard shift at the Salvation Army church. There were about fifty passengers sleeping on mattresses on the church floor and Shaw was there in case someone needed something during the night. She was happy to volunteer. She'd already opened her home and allowed anyone who wanted to clean up to come over and use her shower. The hard part, she soon realized, was keeping enough clean towels on hand. For two days her washer and dryer seemed to be in constant use.

Sitting in the darkened church, Shaw was happy for the peace and quiet. Most of the passengers assigned to stay in the church were asleep by midnight, but she knew a few of the men had gone down to the Moosehead Lounge for something to drink. She would have been able to get a little sleep herself if it hadn't been for the telephone ringing. Every hour a woman called looking for her son, Bill Fitzpatrick. She'd been told he was staying at the church. After gently waking all of the men in church to see if they were Fitzpatrick, Shaw realized he must be one of the guys who was down at the pub.

She called down to the Moosehead and had Fitzpatrick paged, but no one answered. Finally, around 3 A.M., Fitzpatrick arrived at the church. As soon as Shaw heard the door open, the sixty-four-year-old woman pounced.

"Just where have you been?" she scolded.

She didn't even give him a chance to answer.

"And who do you think you are keeping me up half the

night talking to your mother? Did you even realize your mother was worried about you?"

As Shaw berated him, the thirty-eight-year-old Fitzpatrick just stood there with his head hanging low. For those inside the church, it was a marvelous show. Here was this little old woman scolding this fellow who must have been at least a foot taller. As they like to say in these parts, she was "giving him the devil."

"Now you go give your mother a call," Shaw wrapped up. "Right now."

As Fitzpatrick skulked away, several of the other passengers applauded.

▮

After working thirty-eight hours without any sleep, Gary Vey was beat. The president and chief executive officer of the Gander International Airport Authority, he is the man in charge at the airport. Unfortunately, on September 11, Vey wasn't in Gander; he was attending an international conference of airport leaders in Montreal. Ironically, one of the main topics that had been discussed was airport security.

The images of planes being used as weapons left everyone at the conference sickened. And with airspace closed over all of North America, they were stranded at a time when their own airports were dealing with an unprecedented crisis. Rather than waiting for airspace to open so he could fly back to Gander, Vey rented a car and drove more than six hundred miles to the eastern edge of Nova Scotia, where he caught a ferry for a six-hour boat ride across Cabot Strait to the Newfoundland town of Port aux Basques. From there he had an eight-hour drive to Gander.

He drove straight to the airport, and when he arrived

Wednesday afternoon, he was proud to see how well his staff, and for that matter the entire town, had responded to this emergency. His second-in-command, Geoff Tucker, was running the airport's command center and dealing with all of the airlines. Vey left Tucker in charge of the command center while he dealt with other problems as they came up. By about four o'clock in the morning, however, he was starting to wear down. He decided to go home, shower, and catch a couple of hours' sleep before returning to the terminal to handle the next crisis.

Not wanting to wake his wife, he quietly showered in the hallway bathroom and decided to sleep in their guest bedroom. The room was dark as he dropped his towel and climbed into bed, wearing nothing more than wet hair and a weary expression on his face.

And that's when he realized he wasn't alone. He was in bed with a seventy-year-old woman from Fort Worth, Texas, whom Vey's wife, Patsy, had befriended at one of the shelters and decided to take home. Remarkably, the woman was still asleep. Vey gingerly stood up, covered himself with his towel, and retreated to his own bedroom.

"We've got company, I see," he told his wife when they both awoke the next morning.

"Yes," she said, "that's a lovely lady from one of the flights."

She told her husband she couldn't stand the thought of this old woman spending a night sleeping on the floor of a classroom at Gander Academy. So she'd brought her home and tried to show her a good time. Well, he said with a laugh, he almost showed her more than that.

DAY THREE

Thursday

September 13

CHAPTER ELEVEN

Alexandria Loper gets some rest.

Courtesy of Bruce MacLeod

Bright and early Thursday morning, Bruce and Susan MacLeod invited the Lopers and the Wakefields over to their home to use their computer and send e-mails to friends and family. The MacLeods were anxious to help in any way possible, even if it meant placing their own lives on hold for a few days. Susan's birthday came and went on the twelfth without much fanfare because they were both volunteering at the Lions Club. And they were prepared to do the same on Monday if the passengers were still around, even though Monday was also their thirtieth wedding anniversary. There would be time enough to celebrate later, they decided.

The MacLeods "come from aways," as the locals like to say, meaning they were from the mainland of Canada, a town called Moncton in New Brunswick. They had moved to Gander only four years before, when Bruce was transferred to Newfoundland for work. He was an air-traffic controller out at the ATC. Susan was the town's Avon lady. Their jobs gave them the flexibility to take lots of time off and travel. Their two kids were grown and living back in New Brunswick.

Beth Wakefield couldn't help but appreciate the MacLeods' warmth and friendship. Walking through the house, she noticed that all of the mattresses in the guest bedrooms had been stripped. Like everyone else in the Lions Club, the MacLeods had stripped their own beds to provide sheets and blankets and pillows for the passengers.

Beth was thirty-four and her husband, Billy, a UPS driver, was forty. They lived in Goodlettsville, a small town about twenty-five minutes north of Nashville. The worst part of being stranded for both of them was being away from their son, Rob. Unlike the little girl, Diana, they'd adopted in Kazakhstan, Rob was their biological child. He was just three years old and had been expecting his parents home on Tuesday. They knew he would be upset that they weren't there as promised.

Both the Lopers and the Wakefields were experiencing something unique. Amid all the chaos, they were trying to bond with their newly adopted daughters. In every adoption, the first days and weeks the parents spend with the child are critical. The Lopers and the Wakefields were having to spend this time living in a shelter, surrounded by strangers, and with a great deal of uncertainty hanging over their heads. Sympathizing with their predicament, the MacLeods had invited the two couples to their home for a few hours. It might not have seemed like a long time, but for the two families it was a godsend.

∎

Deborah Farrar had been asleep only a couple of hours when she woke to see George Neal standing over her and wearing a grin so large it should have hurt. Deb was curled up in a ball on the floor of George's living room. She was cold and tired, and when she looked over at the clock, she saw that it was seven in the morning. George's wife, Edna, was in the kitchen starting to get breakfast ready for her guests. And George just continued to stand over her smiling, taking his eyes off Deb only long enough to look over at Greg, who was also curled up on the floor of his living room.

"Good morning," George said.

Deb knew she would be in for a day of teasing for having brought Greg home with her. But she didn't care.

"George, I'm freezing," she said. "Do you have any blankets?"

By the time Deb and Greg had arrived home from the pub in Gambo, everyone was asleep. Lana and Winnie had taken the guest room and Bill and Mark had claimed the sofas in television room, so Deb and Greg decided to sleep in the living room. As the others woke up, they all greeted Deb with a big smile and an overly friendly "good morning."

Nothing had happened, she assured them. Greg was a perfect gentleman.

∎

Lenny O'Driscoll bounded downstairs to find Rose Sheppard fixing breakfast in her kitchen. O'Driscoll noticed her front door was unlocked. It must have been that way through the night.

"You know, Rose, you are a very trusting person," Lenny said.

"Why do you say that?"

"Because if I had done this in Brooklyn, I would have had my throat cut," he said. Lenny wasn't just referring to the unlocked front door. He was also talking about the way Rose and Doug Sheppard had invited him and his wife, Maria—two complete strangers—into their home.

Rose told him he had been living in the United States too long and needed to get back to Newfoundland more often. Lenny couldn't have agreed more. This unexpected trip had conjured up old feelings about the country he left so long ago.

"You can't beat a Newfie," Lenny was found of saying.

The O'Driscolls and the Sheppards spent all of their time together. Lenny and Doug, in particular, reminisced about Newfoundland. "When a Newfie meets a Newfie," Lenny explained to Maria, "they have lots to talk about."

Lenny had left Newfoundland prior to the 1949 vote to sever its economic ties to England and become a part of Canada. Doug remembered the vote well. He opposed the union, hoping instead that Newfoundland would somehow become a part of the United States. During World War II there were more than 100,000 Americans—mostly military—living in Newfoundland because of its strategic importance. At least 25,000 Newfoundland women married American servicemen back then. The island's bond to America was always much stronger than its link to Canada.

The events of September 11 were only the most recent proof that those bonds are still there. Doug Sheppard took the O'Driscolls out to the memorial the town had built on the spot where the Arrow Air jet crashed, killing 248 members of the 101st Airborne and a crew of eight. The memorial is a larger-than-life sculpture of an unarmed soldier standing atop a massive rock, holding the hands of two small children, each bearing an olive branch.

The olive branch symbolizes the peacekeeping mission in the Sinai from which the soldiers were returning when their plane crashed. The soldier of the sculpture is looking out across Lake Gander and in the direction of Fort Campbell, Kentucky, the home base for the 101st Airborne. Behind him are three flags—the Canadian flag, the American flag, and the flag of Newfoundland. The cost of the memorial was borne by the local Masonic fraternity and its ladies auxiliary.

Also on the site is a cross surrounded by 256 trees that were planted in the field devastated by the impact of the plane. Taken together—the sculpture, the trees, the flags, and the tranquillity of lake—it is a stirring remembrance to those lost.

Designed and dedicated while Sheppard was mayor, the memorial attracts visitors year-round. For Doug Sheppard, visiting the memorial with the O'Driscolls following September 11 gave it an added meaning. And they were not alone. Hundreds of passengers stranded in Gander asked to be taken to the memorial—which is just outside of town—to see the sculpture and the plaque bearing the names of the dead and the flags now lowered to half-mast.

❙

Patsy Vey was on her way to work when she spotted two young women, dressed in flight-attendant uniforms, walking down the street toward the center of town.

"Would you like a ride?" Vey asked, stopping alongside the pair.

"We're going to the shopping mall to buy some clothes," one of the women responded.

"I've got clothes," Vey quickly offered. "I'll be glad to take you back to my house and you can take what you need."

The women thanked her, saying it was wonderfully generous of her, but they wanted to see what they could find in the stores. On the drive to the mall, Vey had another suggestion. "If you're bored tomorrow," she said, "you can take my car sightseeing."

"You want to lend us your car?"

"Why not?" Vey asked. She operates the Sears outlet in town and the car would just be sitting in a parking lot while she went to work.

"But you don't know us."

"You seem like nice girls," she said. "I trust you. Besides, where would you run off to—it's an island."

The women demurred, saying they really couldn't go sightseeing since they had to be ready to leave at any time. Vey told them that if they changed their minds, to come by the Sears outlet and they could take the car. Most of the time, she added, she leaves the keys in the ignition.

∎

After two days of prodding, Beulah Cooper convinced Hannah O'Rourke to leave the Royal Canadian Legion hall for a few hours to come over to her house to shower. Hannah's husband, Dennis, promised he would stay by the phone at the legion hall, and if there was any news about their son Kevin, he would call her immediately at Cooper's home. Normally, Cooper would bring several passengers home from the legion hall to shower. This time she brought only Hannah. Cooper could tell Hannah was exhausted. She wasn't sleeping and the pain of having her son missing for more than forty-eight hours was taking its toll on the sixty-six-year-old woman.

While Hannah showered, Cooper, who had just turned sixty, made a fresh pot of tea. When Hannah emerged from the bathroom the two women sat in the quiet of the Coopers' home and relaxed for a few moments. Cooper had tried talking to Hannah about her own son, who was a volunteer firefighter in Gander, to tell her she understood how a mother worries when her son is in a dangerous job. Hannah didn't want to talk about it. She found it difficult to say much of anything about Kevin.

It was the distance that made waiting unbearable. Although Hannah wouldn't tell Cooper, she wondered if her family on Long Island was actually telling her the truth about Kevin. Maybe rescue workers had already found him, and he was dead, but her family was afraid to tell her while she was far from home.

Before driving back to the legion hall, Cooper gave her guest a quick tour of Gander. Cooper told her about the town's history and showed her the lake and the different sites. Every minute she kept Hannah entertained and her mind off Kevin's being missing, Cooper considered a personal victory.

Of course Hannah never actually took her mind off Kevin, but Cooper's persistence was endearing. Hannah was moved that the other woman would care so much to make the effort. And the time away from the legion had given her a chance to have a little privacy and collect her thoughts. She thanked Cooper for being so understanding. Returning to the legion hall, Hannah asked Dennis if there was any news. There wasn't. They would just have to keep waiting.

∎

On Thursday afternoon Tom Mercer had a few minutes to spare. He'd spent part of his day taking three teenage girls from Iran shopping at the mall and would later come to the assistance of a group of women from Mozambique, but for now he wanted to check in on his new friends Hannah and Dennis O'Rourke.

Mercer and his wife were staying with their son, an auxiliary police officer with the Royal Canadian Mounted Police, and their daughter-in-law, a bookkeeper at the airport. The younger couple had been called in to work during the crisis, so Mercer and Lilian, his wife of forty-four years, drove in from Port Albert to help as well. While Lilian cared for their grandchildren, Mercer enlisted in a volunteer taxi service that had sprung up to help the passengers get around town.

He was glad to help. Watching the towers collapse and the Pentagon burn had filled him with outrage. A former army sergeant, he'd spent twenty-one years in the Canadian military before retiring, and then the next twenty-two years working as an auto mechanic. He'd worked hard all his life and he couldn't understand how someone could deliberately take the lives of so many innocent people and create such suffering for the victims' families. Nowhere could he see the pain more clearly than on the face of Hannah O'Rourke.

Arriving at the Royal Canadian Legion hall, Mercer quickly found Hannah sitting off to the side, crying. He asked her if there was any news about her firefighter son, Kevin. He tried offering the old adage "No news is good news."

Mercer tried talking about other matters. He sat with her and told her about the other passengers he'd met in town. There was the mother and daughter from Spain. It was because of them that he'd been at the church Wednesday night and had met Hannah and Dennis. He'd seen them several times since, and the girl had started describing Mercer as her "Newfie grandfather." Mercer felt like he was making friends in this short period of time that would last a lifetime.

Hannah also listened as Mercer and her nephew Brendan talked about religion. Brendan was an Irish citizen who was spending more and more time in the United States. Brendan asked Mercer if there were problems in Newfoundland between Catholics and Protestants—the way there were in Ireland.

"A long time ago," Mercer said. "Not anymore."

"What changed?" Brendan asked.

"The young people changed things," Mercer said. "When a young man found a young woman that he liked the look of, religion was the last thing on his mind. And if he was lucky enough to catch her, he didn't let anything come between them."

The O'Rourkes certainly didn't allow many things to come between them. Which is why having Hannah and Dennis trapped far away from home during a family tragedy was proving so difficult for everyone. They weren't used to being apart.

Since the Trade Center towers had collapsed, family members had gathered at Kevin's home in Cedarhurst, Long Island, to support his wife, Maryann, and their two daughters, seventeen-year-old Jamie and twenty-year-old Corrine. So many people were in the house those first few nights that they had to sleep on the floor in the living room. And it was during those moments when everyone was together that Hannah and Dennis's absence was most felt.

Hannah, in particular, had always been the emotional rock for the family. Her strength was in the details, the day-to-day things that would keep them all going. Whether it was making sure there was food to eat or tending to the grandchildren or keeping everyone in the family informed about a particular event, Hannah instinctively knew what needed to be done during a family emergency.

Most of all, though, the family worried how the separation was affecting Hannah and Dennis's ability to cope with their son being missing. They thanked God that Brendan and his girlfriend were with them. They knew Brendan was a real Irish character who could brighten their spirits. And they were relieved to hear there was a church only a few blocks from their shelter. They all knew how much Hannah's faith meant to her. It was no coincidence, after all, that on his days off, Kevin would help patients in the hospital take Communion. He was his mother's son.

They envisioned the way Hannah was probably occupying her time. In lighter moments, they couldn't help but picture her in this remote locale, slowly imposing her will upon the people of Gander. If she's there more than a week, they'd say and laugh, she'll end up being elected mayor. Patricia imagined her mother focusing all of her energy on cleaning or cooking, as she normally did in a crisis.

"Every home in Gander will be spotless by the time she leaves," Patricia would say, while the rest of the family laughed and nodded in agreement.

Nevertheless, they wanted Hannah and Dennis home. Desperate for a solution, they were hoping that Hillary Clinton's Senate office might be able to arrange a special flight for Hannah and Dennis to bring them home immediately. There was little, however, the former first lady could do.

Their only link would remain the telephone.

By now everyone in the legion hall knew Hannah and Dennis and the pain they were experiencing. As soon as Patricia and Maryann or anyone else from the family called, whoever picked up the phone in the legion hall would offer a kind word—"We're praying for all of you" or "Don't worry, we're taking good care of your folks"—and would then run to get them.

There was rarely anything new to tell Hannah or Dennis, which made the calls especially painful. Patricia, though, would try to be encouraging. She would cite news reports of people being pulled alive from the rubble. Nearly all of these reports eventually turned out to be false, but at the time it gave Patricia something hopeful to tell her mother. "They're finding people, Ma," she'd say. "They're getting people out. They're going to find Kevin."

Maryann was no less emphatic during her conversations with Hannah and Dennis.

"They are going to have to prove to me that he's dead," Maryann told Hannah. "They're going to have to find his body before I believe it."

CHAPTER TWELVE

Following the news at the Lions Club.

Flying down the highway, lights flashing and sirens blaring away, the fire truck was on a special mission. There weren't enough new toys in Gander for all of the children from the stranded planes, so the engine was sent on an emergency run to Grand Falls, fifty-five miles west of town. Inside the truck, Susan O'Donnell, the general manager of the Canadian Tire store in Gander, could barely contain her glee. Since Tuesday afternoon, her employees had been doing everything they could think of to help the passengers. And her company was backing them each step of the way.

No sooner had the first planes started to land in Gander than O'Donnell received a phone call from her bosses telling her she had carte blanche to donate everything in the store, if necessary, to the relief effort. "Anything the passengers need that you can provide, please do it," she was instructed. Money was not to be an issue. The costs would be covered by the chain's charitable organization, Foundation for Families. In fact, if another store had something the passengers needed, and that store had reached its limit in terms of donations, then O'Donnell was authorized to go in and buy it for the passengers. It was like a scene right out of *Miracle on 34th Street.*

Over the first few days, Canadian Tire donated almost $20,000 in its own merchandise and spent another $10,000 in other stores, including its chief competitor, Wal-Mart. Normally, O'Donnell can't even bring herself to say Wal-Mart's name aloud, referring to it instead as "that store." For her, Wal-Mart is "that W-word." In an emergency, however, there was no time for rivalries.

Canadian Tire donated sleeping bags, air mattresses, blankets, and bottles of water. One of the first things it donated, though, were toys. One of the firefighters in town realized there were a lot of kids among the passengers and wanted to give each of them a small toy to play with when they came off the plane. He contacted O'Donnell and Susanne Gillingham, the store manager, to see if they could help. Logistically, it would have been difficult to hand the toys out at the airport, so they worked out a plan to have the toys delivered to the various shelters. Canadian Tire sells toys only during Christmas, so its stock in Gander was fairly limited in early September. O'Donnell discovered, however, a warehouse full of toys in Grand Falls. When she explained the situation, the fire department lent her a truck and a driver, and off they went.

O'Donnell had one rule for the toys: nothing violent. No war toys. No guns. Not now, not with everything that had happened on September 11. Instead, O'Donnell loaded up on dolls and stuffed animals and board games and trucks and race cars. She even managed to find a few handheld computer games. She made sure that every toy that needed batteries had them. They filled up the back of the fire truck and raced home to Gander. The fire truck went from shelter to shelter, handing out toys to kids who would come running to greet them. Each day it made a loop of the shelters to make sure none of the kids was missed. Members of Gander's volunteer fire department took turns going to the different schools, churches, and lodges so they could see the look on the kids' faces when they pulled up. O'Donnell wasn't sure how many toys they gave away or how much it cost. She just liked the feeling of being a Newfie Mrs. Claus.

❚

After a peaceful night sleeping in their tent, Sara Wood and Lisa Zale awoke in time for breakfast at the Knights of Columbus. Afterward they returned to their tent to do a little reading. They had picked up a whole stack of trashy magazines during their excursions about town the day before. Then it was down to the community center. The center doubles as an ice rink where hockey games are held, and the locker rooms had showers where passengers could wash up. A large contingent of teenage girls in town volunteered to work shifts at the center, keeping the place tidy and handing out towels and soap and shampoo.

After cleaning up, Wood and Zale went shopping for

clothes at Wal-Mart, had a manicure and a pedicure at a beauty salon, and then swung by the Comfort Inn, where they knew their flight crew was staying. They found a couple of flight attendants and had lunch with them at Jungle Jim's. The crew members had no idea when their flight was going to leave, they told the women. Wood and Zale weren't too worried. They were starting to enjoy their time in Gander. For Zale in particular, it was a nice break from her three kids, two boys and a girl, ranging in age from nine to fifteen. There was no reason why her husband, Mark, couldn't handle things for a few days. By the second day, though, Mark was calling the Knights of Columbus regularly.

"I'd like to speak to Lisa Zale," he'd say.

"Who?"

"The girl in the tent," he'd respond. "She's one of the tent girls."

"Oh, okay, hold on, I'll get her." He called so often with questions for his wife that folks started recognizing his voice.

Since there was a chance of rain Thursday night, the women walked back to Wal-Mart to pick up a couple of tarps to further insulate their tent. Everywhere they went around town, they brought their shopping cart, filling it with items they might need. People offered them rides, but they liked the freedom of walking. When they started lining their tent with the additional tarp, the other passengers told them they were definitely deranged if they were going to sleep outside in a tent during a rainstorm. But Wood and Zale loved their tent. They even bought a little chandelier for the inside. Well, not exactly a chandelier. It was just a flashlight they hung from the roof of the tent. As far as they were concerned, though, it was a chandelier, and nobody was going to tell them otherwise. And tonight, when the rain started to pelt their little green tent, they would put on the pajamas they bought at Wal-Mart, climb into their sleeping bags, read their trashy magazines, and eat left-over junk food. It would be a regular slumber party. The only thing missing, they thought, were the curlers to do each other's hair, and a working telephone to make crank calls to boys.

|

There are reportedly only 144 Bonobo monkeys in captivity, including Cosana and her traveling companion, Unga. They'd been on their way from the Dierenpark Planckendael Zoo in Belgium to a zoo in Ohio when they were unexpectedly detoured into Gander. Cosana and Unga are part of an endangered species found in the Democratic Republic of the Congo, formerly Zaire, in Central Africa. Only twenty years ago there was thought to be 100,000 Bonobos. Today, according to a project known as the Bonobo Initiative, there are fewer than 3,000 in Africa.

Genetically speaking, no other animal is closer to a human being than a Bonobo monkey. Cousin to the chimpanzee, Bonobos even look more like humans than any other ape. And Bonobos are closer genetically to humans than they are to gorillas.

Thanks to Doc Tweedie's efforts, the Bonobos were allowed off their plane and settled into the same hangar with the cats and dogs. For five days, their handler, Harry, rarely left the monkeys alone. Harry was so afraid of Unga and Cosana escaping that he wouldn't allow them out of their traveling pens. Not even to wash out their cages.

From the standpoint of cleanliness, this wasn't a problem. After going to the bathroom, the Bonobos actually picked up their tiny turds and pass them through the bars of the cage to Harry, who would then dispose of them. Cosana even took great care in tidying up around her cage. Each morning, she tossed to the ground all of the hay in her cage; then Harry held up a fresh batch of straw, and Cosana carefully selected the pieces she wanted for her bedding. Unga was less particular and would throw the hay around his cage, often making quite a mess.

The Bonobos were kept only a few feet from the portable kennels that held the dogs and cats. The monkeys seemed absolutely fascinated by the other animals, particularly the dogs. After a while they even tried to imitate the barking sounds of the dogs. Whether the pair was attempting to mimic or to mock the dogs no one could tell.

Watching Cosana and Unga was a real treat for Tweedie, who spends most of his time around the region's livestock. He peppered Harry with questions about the animals. Tweedie appreciated Harry's devotion to the animals, but also felt sorry for the handler, because he was actually sleeping at the airport alongside the monkeys. After a couple of nights, the veterinarian finally convinced Harry to come home with him for dinner. Two hours later Harry was back at the airport caring for the animals.

❚

Patsy Vey had trouble concentrating at work and decided to spend the day helping the stranded passengers instead. A family from Saudi Arabia had just finished showering in her home when her phone rang. Early on she—along with a few hundred other people—had placed her name on a list of folks who would be willing to allow passengers to shower in their homes. Rather than wait for them to get to her name on the list, she had gone out earlier that day to one of the shelters and found a family anxious for a chance to use her bathroom.

Now the folks working through the phone list were calling

to see if she could let an elderly couple shower and get cleaned up at her house. Vey couldn't bring herself to say no. Instead, she told them she'd be right down. The couple's name was John and Marie Uncle, and once Vey picked them up, she realized she couldn't bring the Uncles back to her house. She hadn't properly cleaned her bathroom after her most recent guests. Worst of all, she had no fresh towels left.

Suddenly it hit her. She'd bring them to her friend's home. Sure enough, when she called, the friend was happy to oblige. "Come on over," Vey's friend exclaimed. On the way to her friend's house, Vey discovered that the Uncles were from Alexandria, Virginia. Vey's daughter, Kelly, lived in Alexandria. "What a splendid coincidence," she said. As they continued to talk, the Uncles said their daughter, Peggy, was upset that her parents were marooned in a town she had never heard of before. Vey told the Uncles she had the perfect solution for Peggy's worries. Vey would have Kelly call Peggy and allay her fears. That night, Kelly Vey went one step better. She met Peggy in person and assured her over dinner that there wasn't a better place in the world to be trapped in than Gander.

CHAPTER THIRTEEN

Royal Canadian Sea Cadets helping out at the Lions Club.

Werner Baldessarini found himself in a place he'd never been before, a place he never imagined he would visit in his lifetime—the men's underwear department of Wal-Mart.

For most folks in Gander, Wal-Mart has everything they'll ever need. Since the first planes landed on Tuesday, however, the store had been overrun with passengers, and by Thursday the shelves were starting to look a bit bare, particularly in the underwear section. It was one thing, apparently, to wear T-shirts or pants or dresses donated to the local shelters during this crisis. It was an entirely different matter to wear secondhand underwear. Many of the stranded passengers who accepted assistance drew the line at accepting hand-me-down briefs.

And it was certainly a line Baldessarini had no intention of even approaching. In his twenty-seven years with Hugo Boss, first as a buyer, then as a designer, and now as the company's chairman, he had helped shape the world's image of what it meant to dress for success. Through the eighties and nineties, a Hugo Boss power suit, with its classic lines and dark tones, set the standard by which all other clothiers were measured. But it wasn't just the suits. Hugo Boss designed shirts, slacks, leather jackets, shoes, boots, sandals, sunglasses, cologne, and yes, underwear. Cotton briefs, boxer shorts, and boxer briefs. All heralded for their quality and marquee name.

Baldessarini himself was no less stylish.

As one would expect, he was a walking advertisement for his company, dressing head to toe in Hugo Boss apparel. The cashmere suit he'd worn for the flight from Frankfurt to New York was from a special line of clothes the company produces under a signature label bearing his name. And while the suit was holding up quite well during extended wear and adverse conditions, common decency demanded a change of underwear.

Entering Wal-Mart, Baldessarini walked between the smiling greeter in the blue vest and a row of shopping carts, past a display of beer coolers and lawn furniture, and around several racks of T-shirts bearing the likenesses of professional wrestlers and NASCAR drivers. The men's underwear wasn't actually in a department of its own in the store, more like an aisle, containing several metal tiers of shelves. He found the appropriate size and style, and then stood in line and paid at the checkout stand.

When he returned to the school, he showered and

changed. He immediately felt uncomfortable. The waistband, the material, the design—it was all wrong.

Baldessarini was living through his very own version of the Hans Christian Andersen story of "The Princess and the Pea." This wasn't snobbery as much as it was a realization of the superiority of his product. After all, a person who is used to filet mignon certainly notices when someone tries to pass off a Salisbury steak in its place.

Luckily, help was on the way.

Having also worn the same clothes for the better part of three days, Deborah Farrar, Lana Etherington, and Winnie House were anxious to go shopping. Since there really wasn't a place for them to shop in Gambo, George Neal offered to drive them all into Gander. Bill Cash, Mark Cohen, and Greg Curtis went along as well. And like everyone else, they ended up at Wal-Mart.

Winnie was browsing through what was left of the women's underwear in the store when she noticed a young girl who was about ten staring at her. Since arriving in Newfoundland, Winnie had been very conscious of the fact that she was often the only black person around. At one point she had asked George if there were any black people living in Gambo. "No," he said, shaking his head, "not really."

Even if she hadn't been black, Winnie wasn't the type of person who was capable of just blending into a crowd. Her shoes made her almost six feet tall. She was wearing Dolce & Gabbana designer jeans and her hair brushed the small of her back. Winnie looked over again at the young girl. The child was saying something to her mother.

"Go ahead," the mother told the girl. "It's okay."

The girl walked over. Winnie could tell from the mother's accent that they were locals.

"Excuse me," the girl said. "Can I have your autograph?"

Winnie was flabbergasted. "I'm really a nobody," she replied.

The child's mother smiled and told her it didn't matter. "You're somebody to her," she said.

A little embarrassed, Winnie agreed, and the mother dug through her purse for a piece of paper. The child asked if she could touch Winnie's hair.

"Of course," Winnie said. The child stroked it gently as Winnie signed her name, along with a few Xs and Os, for hugs and kisses.

"Thank you," the child said, leaving with her mother.

Winnie was so moved she wanted to cry. Throughout her stay in Newfoundland, she was always greeted with such warmth. In all her travels around the world, it was one of the few times she was made to feel her skin color didn't matter.

Outside the Wal-Mart, Deb walked over to Greg, who was shaking his head and looking disappointed.

"All they have left in the men's section is extra-small and thong underwear," he said.

"Really," Deb said gleefully. "Let me see."

Before she could reach into his bag, he told her he was just kidding. Leaving the mall and heading back to Gambo, Deb realized that she really liked Greg. And she could tell he liked her as well. After being thrown together the night before, they were now getting to know a little bit more about each other. Where were they born? Where did they grow up? How large were their families? Where did they go to school?

Because they were spending so much time together, it felt as if they were compressing the normal dating cycle, so that by their second night together it seemed like they had known each other a lot longer, and they were growing close. But there also wasn't as much pressure on them as there might have been since they were always in a fairly large group, with George, Edna, Winnie, Bill, Lana, and Mark usually around.

|

Not even an international tragedy can slow down a determined personal assistant trying to please his or her boss.

Inside the Frankfurt headquarters of Hugo Boss, the full resources of the company were being tapped to aide their stranded chairman. On Tuesday, company executives thought Baldessarini's flight was being diverted to Toronto, so they dispatched the president of Hugo Boss's Canadian subsidiary, Les Minion, to the airport to greet him. After two hours of waiting, Minion learned that the flight had been diverted to Gander.

On Wednesday, Hugo Boss chairman Werner Baldessarini contacted his corporate offices to let them know he was safe and where he would be staying for the foreseeable future. Baldessarini's first concern was making sure that all his people in New York were safe. And they were. The remainder of Fashion Week had been canceled and Hugo Boss would have to delay the release of its spring collection—a decision that cost the company almost $2 million. Given everything that was happening in the United States, the collection and the money were merely trivial details to Baldessarini.

By the time Baldessarini called in, his staff was already making plans for his rescue. Hugo Boss is a major sponsor of the McLaren Formula One race team. The principal owner of the team is Mansour Ojjeh, a wealthy Saudi Arabian businessman. When Ojjeh learned his good friend Baldessarini was stranded in Gander, he offered to send his personal jet to Newfoundland to pick him up. As his staff coordinated these efforts, Baldessarini mentioned the uncomfortable bind he was in—literally—regarding his underwear. Snapping into action, his assistants in Germany once again contacted Minion to see if this situation could be rectified.

Minion knew exactly what to do. The closest Hugo Boss outlet to Gander was Byron's, a men's clothing store in St. John's, about two hundred miles away. Minion contacted the owner, Byron Murphy, and asked if he could send one of his store clerks to Gander with a CARE package for someone.

"Who's out there?" Murphy asked.

"It's Werner," Minion replied.

"Werner Baldessarini?"

"That's right."

Murphy couldn't believe his ears. In Murphy's world of fashion retail, Baldessarini was the equivalent of a movie star. Murphy prided himself on owning the premier men's clothing store in St. John's, and, for that matter, in all of Newfoundland. He had over 3,000 square feet spread over two floors in a redbrick building in the historic section of St. John's. He carried an assortment of name brands—Polo, Manzoni, Lipson, Cambridge, Greg Norman. The Hugo Boss line, however, was one of his bestsellers.

Since opening the store ten years before, he had always dreamed of meeting someone of Baldessarini's stature, but was never part of that in-crowd that went to the big fashion shows and rubbed elbows with such icons. Murphy knew he'd regret it his entire life if he let this moment slip away.

"I'll go, I'll do it," Murphy volunteered.

Minion gave him a list of items. Murphy packed an assortment of shirts, pants, socks, and underwear—all Hugo Boss, of course. Unsure of the chairman's preferred style, Murphy selected both boxers and briefs. In addition to a change of clothes, Minion asked Murphy to assemble a basket of food and gave him suggestions on bottles of wine and types of breads and cheeses. Murphy picked up several nice bottles of Merlot—a couple from Australia, one from Chile, and another from Italy. He also found a lovely Gouda and some Brie and a few loaves of French bread.

The drive from St. John's is nearly three hours, and Murphy didn't arrive until almost 6 P.M. The thirty-nine-year-old Murphy didn't have any problem finding the school, Gander Collegiate, where Baldessarini was staying. Murphy had been born in Gander. As soon as he arrived, he went to the school office and had Baldessarini paged. Within minutes, he spotted the chairman emerging from the school's gym. He recognized him from his pictures in the catalogs.

"Mr. Baldessarini," Murphy said, a bit awestruck, "my name is Byron Murphy."

"Pleased to meet you," Baldessarini said. "Thanks for driving out."

Murphy led him outside to his car and the packages he'd brought with him. The chairman was a bit embarrassed. He told Murphy that while he was grateful for his efforts, he couldn't accept the baskets of food and wine. He wanted to eat what everyone else was eating.

Baldessarini thought about offering the items to the town's relief effort but decided against it. He was afraid his donation would suggest that the food the people in Gander were offering the passengers wasn't good enough. Baldessarini's voice was filled with emotion when he described to Murphy the efforts of everyone in town to aide the passengers, particularly the women, who seemed to be cooking around the clock. He didn't want to risk doing something that might offend these fine folks, he explained.

"Take them back with you," he told Murphy.

Not wanting to be a complete masochist, though, he did take the underwear. Both the boxers and the briefs. Leaving the other items in the car, Murphy and Baldessarini went back inside the school, where the chairman showed him around and introduced him to some of his new friends from the plane. In the cafeteria, they had a soda and talked a little men's retail. Baldessarini briefed Murphy on the spring line and asked him questions about his store. How large was it? Which items sold best? Which didn't? Murphy thought Baldessarini seemed genuinely interested in his opinions.

In the background, a television was tuned to CNN, and the two men talked about the terrorist attacks. After a couple of hours Murphy announced that he'd better start the drive home to St. John's. Baldessarini walked him out, thanked him for the clothes, and invited to come to Europe, where he could tour the Hugo Boss headquarters and attend one of the company's fashion shows.

As he drove home, it all seemed so surreal for Murphy. Was he dreaming or did he just spend two hours in a high school cafeteria in Gander, Newfoundland, talking to the chairman of Hugo Boss about fashion and world politics after delivering him an emergency supply of underwear? It was no dream, and in the morning, when he opened his store and laid out the cheese and wine for his customers, he had quite a story to tell them.

▌

Jessica Naish had never seen so much food. Since she'd been bused to the volunteer fire department in Gambo on Wednesday afternoon, hardly an hour had passed without someone from town walking in with another tray or dish of food for the passengers. Casseroles. Stews. Salads. Homemade pies and cakes. Fresh-baked cookies. It wasn't possible to sample it all.

Naish was a passenger on Continental Flight 5. An American, she'd been living in Cheddar, England, and was on her way to Houston to visit family and friends. On the plane, she'd met two men, Paul Moroney and Peter Ferris. Although she was sure their paths had never crossed before their ill-fated flight, Naish couldn't help but feel she had met them before. There was something very familiar about the two, but she wasn't sure what it was. Until they told her what they did for a living. They were professional Beatles impersonators and performed in a group called the Beatles Band.

Moroney portrayed John Lennon.

Ferris played George Harrison.

They both wore their hair in mop-top fashion, the love-me-do haircuts of the early Beatles. Even their clothes harkened back to that era. Ferris was wearing a dark green suit with a black turtleneck sweater and Moroney was dressed in a gray suit and a dark button-down shirt. The rest of the band was back in England. Moroney and Ferris were going to Texas to visit friends they made during a recent series of concerts the group played in Lubbock. The birthplace of Buddy Holly was crazy for the faux Fab Four. The group had sold out shows in February, and then again throughout most of the summer. During the Fourth of July weekend, they appeared with a 120-piece orchestra in an outdoor concert in front of 100,000 people.

Naish was fascinated with the stories Moroney and Ferris were telling her. As they explained it, they weren't some Beatles cover band. They were a tribute band. "We try to become for people what the essence of the Beatles were," Ferris told her. Naish was dying to hear them perform.

That wasn't going to happen, both men assured her. At least not here in Newfoundland. Ferris was thirty-four years old and had been born in Belfast. He'd grown up during the "troubles," as the fighting in Northern Ireland is often called. As a boy, he often saw people who were traumatized by the unrest. It had a unique effect on people. He saw that same look on the faces of his fellow passengers in Gambo as they watched the news reports from the United States. He'd seen enough scared people for one lifetime and, instead of huddling inside, was spending time instead down by the river, which was a short walk from the fire station. It was quiet and peaceful there.

CHAPTER FOURTEEN

A Moldovan family cooking at the Baptist church.

Oh my God! Did you see that!"

Anna Lee Gosse turned quickly to see who was screaming. A ninth-grade teacher at Lewisporte Middle School, the twenty-five-year-old was afraid something terrible had happened on the street. As she ran in the direction of the man's voice, she could still hear him screaming, "Did you see that! Did you see that!"

The middle school sits on the main road that runs through

Lewisporte and divides the town down the middle. As her eyes focused on the man making all of the commotion, Gosse slowed down; she could see that he was also laughing. He was pointing at a large truck, which had stopped in the middle of road to allow several people to cross.

Based upon the man's accent, Gosse surmised he was from New York or New Jersey. "He just stopped," said the man, with the same sort of amazement that the children of Fatima must have felt upon seeing the Blessed Virgin.

The man looked around to make sure others had seen this miracle. "No crosswalk, no stop sign, no traffic light," he bellowed. "He just stopped."

Gosse and another teacher watched the man for a few seconds. These Americans truly are strange folks, she thought, and then turned to go back inside the school.

▐

Seventeen-year-old Tara Boyde had never met royalty before and she wasn't sure how to react when one of the passengers told her that he was a prince. He was from somewhere in the Middle East, but she couldn't remember the name of the country. He had long flowing robes and his wife didn't speak English. They were traveling on a US Air flight out of Paris with their four-year-old son, and were on their way to the United States, where the boy was scheduled to have surgery. They also had a nurse who was caring for the boy.

They had been taken to the Salvation Army camp about twenty minutes outside of Gander, and the prospect of sleeping in a cabin in the middle of the woods was not sitting well with His Royal Highness. He was demanding to be taken to a hotel, but Boyde explained that this wasn't possible. She suspected he was worried about his son. She didn't know why the child was scheduled to have surgery. She assumed it was serious.

Boyde attends the Salvation Army church and had volunteered to help as soon as she heard about the planes arriving in Gander. She helped the prince and his family settle into a cabin and then scrounged up a bunch of toys for their little boy. The prince was still angry, but Boyde didn't let it bother her. This must be very hard on them, she thought.

Most of the passengers who were taken to the Salvation Army camp enjoyed it because it was so isolated. There was only one small television set in the entire facility. As a result of this, passengers occupied their time swimming in the lake, canoeing, taking hikes, and playing soccer and baseball.

▌

Pam Coish, the principal for Lewisporte Middle School, was sitting in her office when one of the passengers knocked on her door. Coish recalled the passenger's name was Denise and she was traveling with a group of people aboard Continental Flight 45 from Milan to Newark. The first day they arrived in Lewisporte, one of the men traveling with Denise, a fellow named Gordon, asked if he could use the school's computers. "I have a small business to run," he explained. Coish told him all of the passengers were welcome to use the computers.

Coish invited Denise into her office.

"Pam, I just wanted to say how grateful we are for everything you've done," Denise said. She then handed the principal her business card. Coish read it carefully. Her name was Denise Gray-Felder, vice-president of administration and communications for the Rockefeller Foundation. The man with a small business to run, Gray-Felder explained, was Gordon Conway, president of the foundation.

The Rockefeller Foundation is one of the largest philanthropic groups on the planet, overseeing a $3 billion endowment and providing almost $200 million in grants every year to needy organizations throughout the world. Conway and Gray-Felder, along with four other executives from the foundation, had been flying home from a board of directors meeting in Italy when their plane was diverted to Gander.

Conway, Gray-Felder, and the others were so impressed with the outpouring of support from the community that they wanted to do something for the school. They came up with the idea of providing new computers for the school and the 317 students who go there each year. The thirty-five machines in the computer lab were hopelessly out-of-date—the students were still using 133s, for goodness' sake—and the group thought a onetime grant to purchase new equipment was in order.

"We'd like to replace your computer lab," Gray-Felder told Coish.

The principal was flabbergasted. She had no idea they'd been running the Rockefeller Foundation from one of her classrooms. And she felt funny about accepting a gift from any of the passengers.

"We didn't do it for the money," Coish told Gray-Felder. She told the vice-president it wasn't necessary for the foundation to do anything.

"This is something we want to do," Gray-Felder insisted. "And we'll do it whether you want it or not."

Gray-Felder had no intention of allowing Coish to demure. Her time in Lewisporte had been such a wondrous experience. After thirty hours on the plane, she and the 115 other passengers aboard Continental Flight 45 had been taken by bus to Lewisporte and dropped off in front of the Philadelphia Tabernacle Pentecostal Church Wednesday afternoon.

Gray-Felder was a bit leery at first. She imagined sleeping on hard wooden pews. Luckily the benches were padded. At the end of each pew was a stack of blankets and several toothbrushes and tubes of toothpaste.

Across the street was the middle school. The passengers were told they could shower and eat over there as well use the phones and the school's computers. It was Conway who dove into work sooner than the other foundation members. The foundation has offices and programs around the world, so a lot of its work is done over the Internet. Gray-Felder and the others soon followed suit, first letting everyone know they were safe and then falling into the rhythm of reading reports, reviewing grant proposals, and working on budgets.

Immersing themselves in the mundane was a good way for them to occupy their minds with something other than the horrors of September 11. While Conway and some of the other executives used a few of the school's computers, Gray-Felder had her laptop with her. She had a problem, however, connecting it to the school's phone system, so one of the teachers, Judy Freake, allowed her to use an outlet in her home.

There was nothing the passengers needed that the people in town weren't prepared to provide. Each night the strandees were there, several women from town would stay up until two in the morning washing loads of towels so the passengers would have fresh towels each morning when they woke up.

Gray-Felder knew people had donated the towels from their own homes, and she asked one of the women how everyone was going to reclaim their towels once the passengers left. The woman looked at her as if it was an odd question.

"It doesn't matter," she said.

The selflessness of the townspeople gave Gray-Felder chills.

Their first night in Lewisporte, Gray-Felder had had trouble sleeping and around 3 A.M. spotted several men from town, including Pastor Russell Bartlett, sitting by the entrance of the church. She asked why they were still awake.

"We thought it was important to watch over you," the pastor explained, "and make sure nothing happened to you while you slept."

Conway and the others were all touched by similar experiences. There was a pub near the school where the Rockefeller folks would gather for what they jokingly referred to as "quasi—staff meetings," and all of them agreed they should find a way to repay both the school and the church. When Gray-Felder knocked on Coish's door to deliver the news, she also explained that if there was a more pressing need at the school, the foundation would leave it up to the principal and her staff to decide how best to use their money. Coish said she wanted to speak to her vice-principal and would let her know in a couple of weeks.

After Gray-Felder left, Coish decided to keep the news from the rest of her staff in case the foundation people later changed their minds about the grant. She was afraid of getting her staff's hopes up too high.

When Gray-Felder met with Pastor Bartlett at the church, he was also dumbfounded. She said the foundation would like to do something nice for the church. Was there a project or a program the foundation could support? Like Coish, the pastor said he wanted time to think about it.

∎

A young couple from one of the planes was walking down a residential street in Gander, carrying a small child, when they heard a woman yell out, "Wait! Wait!" She had stuck her head out her front door and motioned for the young couple to please stop and that she would be right back. The couple wasn't sure what was happening but patiently waited to find out.

After a couple of minutes the woman came running out of her house with a stroller. "Here, why don't you use this?" she asked. There was no use carrying their child, the woman explained, when she had a perfectly good stroller they could borrow.

The young couple tried to tell her it wasn't necessary. Besides, they weren't sure when they were leaving or how they would be able to get the stroller back to her. The woman told her it didn't matter. Her kids were grown and she didn't need it any longer. "Take it," she insisted. "I want to help."

▐

The crew of Lufthansa 400 stayed at the Sinbad Hotel, along with ten other flight crews. There was little for them to do. Captain Reinhard Knoth divided his crew into two groups. The first would be responsible for making sure the plane was ready to fly as soon as they were given the clearance to leave. They needed to make sure the plane was clean, that there was food and water on board, and that the ground workers in Gander received any assistance they might need. The second group would make sure the passengers were okay and being properly treated. Knoth placed himself in that second group.

Knoth felt a deep sense of responsibility for his passengers. Whether it took six hours or six days to get them from Frankfurt to New York, they were still *his* passengers and he was obliged to look after them.

Every morning he'd set out from his hotel to walk to Gander Collegiate, the high school where the passengers from his flight were staying. Knoth didn't mind walking, the weather was beautiful, and it gave him a chance to think. Or at least it would have, if the folks in Gander hadn't been so friendly. Without fail, Knoth would walk no more than two or three blocks before one of the townspeople pulled up alongside him and offered him a ride to wherever he was going. The same would happen when he walked back to the hotel from the school.

On his visits to the school, the first question every passenger asked him was always: "When are we leaving?" He wished he knew. There was just no way of telling. All he could say to them was that they had to be ready to leave for the airport at a moment's notice.

Knoth spent most of his time at the school. He liked not only the people on his plane but also the folks who worked at the school. He was especially fond of the principal, Jim Pittman. The two men talked at length about life in Gander and life in Germany. Although the school was crowded with people, Knoth found it relaxing. Everyone's spirits remained high, and while they missed being home with loved ones, they were determined to make the best of the situation.

The mood was different back at the hotel. The concept of taking over airplanes and using them as weapons—turning them, in effect, into missiles—was particularly hard to grasp for the people who made their living aboard airplanes. Some pilots and crew members simply locked themselves away, not dealing with anyone. Others tried to find ways to keep busy. At the Sinbad, a copilot for one of the Delta flights took over a conference room and stocked it with alcohol. He dubbed it "The Crew's Lounge." Each night, the "lounge" would fill up, giving personnel from different airlines a chance to meet and talk without any outsiders around. It wasn't that they were trying to be unfriendly, but no one could know what they were going through.

Inside the lounge, Knoth studied his colleagues. They were angry and scared and depressed. Some were physically exhausted, while others were just wrung out emotionally. It didn't particularly matter if any of these men and women personally knew a crew member from one of the hijacked planes. All they needed to know was that it could just as easily have been them. Everyone had a different way of coping. Some crew members carried on like they were on holiday at a swingers' resort. Others made inappropriate jokes about the tragedy. The vast majority, like Knoth, threw themselves into their work by seeing to their passengers.

Knoth was especially concerned about one young member of his crew. This was his first flight to the United States and he just seemed daunted by the events. Knoth tried approaching him, but he refused to talk about it. For the longest time he just wouldn't say anything.

There was genuine fear among the flight crews, especially as they were given notice that their flights were next in line to leave. Rumors were rampant that Canadian authorities were suspicious of some of the passengers, but they didn't have enough proof to keep them from getting back on their planes. Some flight attendants were threatening not to fly if certain Middle Eastern passengers were permitted on the planes. Officials from the RCMP frequently had to assure flight crews that a particular passenger was not a threat.

The fears weren't limited to passengers of Arab descent. In Gambo, the folks in town had posted a long three-foot-wide strip of brown paper on a table for passengers to sign and write comments on before leaving. Several passengers became concerned when they noticed someone had written, "Yahoo, Osama bin Laden. Looks good on you." Nobody was quite sure what the words meant, but it sounded like the person was applauding the terrorist attack. Town officials called the police, and several Mounties arrived to investigate. Gathering all of the passengers together in one room, the Mounties started to ask if anyone knew who wrote the item, when a passenger from Continental Flight 29, which was going from London to Newark, admitted it was him. The young man was from Ireland and he said folks had misunderstood what he meant. He didn't write it as a cheer for bin Laden; rather, he was saying it looked like he was the one responsible.

No matter the man's real intentions—a misunderstanding of an idiomatic expression or just a really stupid thing to write down—the Mounties concluded that the man was not a terrorist. For his own safety, however, Gambo officials kept the man separated from the other passengers, some of whom were irate enough to assault the fellow. Some passengers even believed their flight was being delayed further because of his missive.

When word reached the crew for Continental Flight 29 in Gander, the pilot declared that he would not allow that passenger back on his plane. The Mounties assured the crew that the man was safe. As the plane was preparing to leave, the pilot said the only way he would allow the man back on his plane was if he was handcuffed for the duration of the flight. The Mounties told the pilot and the crew they had no legal authority to place the man in handcuffs; he hadn't committed a crime. By now the Irish fellow was feeling quite embarrassed. He told the pilot and the Mounties that he would voluntarily agree to be handcuffed if he could get on the plane. Like everyone else, he just wanted to go home.

As the man was brought aboard the plane, the other passengers scowled at him. At the last minute the pilot relented. He told the man as long as he remained quiet and didn't bother anyone, he would not have him handcuffed. The man thanked him and the flight proceeded without any problems.

|

Terry Trainor, an investigator with the major crimes section of the Royal Canadian Mounted Police, arrived at the Hotel Gander a little before 5 P.M. on Thursday. Lufthansa Flight 440 was being given clearance to leave that night, but four passengers were missing, and Trainor had come to the hotel to meet with the pilot and his crew. Officers were being dispatched to the various shelters and to check the hospital, and the pilot was concerned that if the missing passengers weren't found soon, it might hurt his chances of getting out that night.

Trainor could tell the pilot was ready to leave. The events in the United States, the uncertainty of their next move, and the stress of being isolated in Gander all contributed to his eagerness to get out as soon as possible. As Trainor was speaking with the pilot, the copilot, and the flight engineer, there was a knock on the pilot's hotel-room door. It was a passenger, though, unfortunately, not one of the missing ones.

The man was American and looked to be ex-military. He was tall and athletic, probably somewhere between forty-five and fifty years old. Trainor could tell he had been drinking, although he didn't appear drunk.

The man told the pilot that he'd been talking to some of the other passengers in the hotel bar and they were worried that once they became airborne, somebody might try to take over the plane as had happened with those flights on the eleventh. Proudly the man declared that he'd come up with a plan to prevent this from happening. He told the pilot he had already recruited three other passengers—big guys, Americans—who were prepared to stand in front of the cockpit door during the flight as guards. All they needed were axes.

Axes?

The man reasoned that if they were going to be called on to fend off a possible terrorist assault, they should be armed with axes. Obviously, they had thought about asking for guns, but ruled this out as being too dangerous. An errant shot might blow out a window and cause the plane to crash, and that would defeat the whole purpose of having guards in the first place. But if a guard had an ax, who would be crazy enough to challenge him?

Trainor looked over to see the pilot's reaction. The man just sighed. He wasn't angry, but he was unable to find the humor in the idea of passing out axes to passengers. He just looked tired and a bit exasperated. The pilot caught Trainor's eye and gave him a look that the investigator interpreted as meaning one thing: *Find my missing passengers and let me get the hell out of here!*

CHAPTER FIFTEEN

One of the pilots talks with his passengers.

By midafternoon, the pilot for Lufthansa Flight 438 arrived at the Lions Club with good news. Rather than flying back to Germany, as many of the passengers had feared, the plane would instead be going on to Dallas. The announcement was greeted with cheers and shouts of thanks.

The passengers would have only a short time to get their belongings together before the buses arrived to take them to the airport. Roxanne and Clark Loper were thrilled. When the buses arrived, the volunteers at the Lions Club formed a line leading to the door. It was like a receiving line at a wedding. As they made their way down the row, hugging and thanking each person, both Roxanne and Beth were surprised by how emotional it was. They had known these people for less than thirty-six hours, but they were already family. Bruce handed Roxanne a piece of paper with his name, phone number, and e-mail address, and told her to call when they arrived safe in Texas.

MacLeod had one more chore before they all left. He had learned that one of the passengers, a nineteen-year-old from India or Pakistan—he wasn't sure which—had spent the last of her traveling money in town. She was on her way to live with relatives in the United States and didn't speak much English. MacLeod pulled the young woman aside and discreetly handed her an American twenty-dollar bill. The young woman seemed confused.

"I wouldn't send my daughter on a plane without any money in her pocket, and I'm not going to send you that way either," he told her.

The woman burst into tears and threw her arms around him.

Once at the airport, passengers were run through a gauntlet of security. They were gone over with a metal detecting wand and patted down as well. From there, they were broken into groups of forty. Each set of passengers was then ushered onto the tarmac, where, alongside their plane, was all of their luggage. It had been removed and screened, but before it would be placed back on the plane, each passenger had to personally identify his or her bags.

Roxanne, Clark, and Alexandria were in the final group. As they pointed out their luggage for the baggage handlers, eighteen-year-old Lisa Cox came running over to Roxanne.

"This plane is going back to Germany," she said excitedly.

"What do you mean?" Roxanne asked.

"It's going back to Germany," Lisa repeated. "That baggage handler over there told me."

Roxanne looked to the member of the ground crew Lisa was pointing at and ran over to him.

"Where is this plane going?" she asked.

"Germany," he said.

"Are you sure?"

"Yeah."

Roxanne was furious. Clark thought it might still be a mistake. Maybe the baggage handler was wrong. He saw the pilot standing near the steps leading up to the plane. "Where are we flying to?" Clark asked.

"Germany," the pilot declared.

"Why did you lie to us?" Clark demanded angrily.

"I didn't know myself until two hours ago," he said.

By now Roxanne was standing alongside Clark and Alexandria.

"Two hours," she hissed. "That was plenty of time to tell us. Why didn't you come into the terminal?" She realized the passengers on the plane had no idea they were heading to Germany. Frustrated that his secret had leaked out, the pilot told Clark and Roxanne to get up the stairs and take their seats.

"What will happen to us when we get to Germany?" Clark asked.

"We'll talk about that on the plane," the pilot said.

"No, we won't," Clark said. "We're not getting on that plane."

During the previous twenty-four hours, as his wife rallied the other passengers to oppose the idea of flying back to Germany, Clark had been fairly ambivalent. If the quickest way to get home was by first flying back to Germany, then he was willing to consider it. He wouldn't have left his wife and child behind, and ultimately he'd probably have deferred to his wife's strong wishes, but it would have been worth a talk with her in private.

Now that he felt lied to by the pilot, there was no way in hell Clark was boarding this flight. Another couple, Tera and Jason Saarista, who were traveling with their two children, overheard the argument between Clark and the pilot. The Saaristas announced that they weren't getting on the plane either. The pilot finally gave up and stormed off. The two families were led back into the airport, placed in a holding area, and placed under armed guard.

The scene on the plane was about to get equally chaotic. Beth and Billy Wakefield were among the first to board the plane and had no idea what was happening outside to Roxanne and Clark. As she settled into her seat, Beth jokingly asked the flight attendant, "Just making sure, we are going to Dallas, aren't we?"

"There will be an announcement once everyone has boarded," the grim-faced flight attendant said.

"Are you saying we're going to Frankfurt?" Beth asked.

"There will be an announcement after everyone is on the plane," the flight attendant repeated.

Beth could feel herself begin to shake. Her husband, Billy, started yelling at the flight attendant and telling other passengers they were going to Germany. In another part of the plane, Lisa Cox was telling her mother and her sister the same thing.

"Let's get off the plane," she pleaded to her mother.

By now word had spread among all of the passengers that the plane was heading for Frankfurt. Some were standing in the aisles, screaming and shouting profanities at the pilot and the crew. Beth was sobbing uncontrollably. Diana was screaming. The pilot was yelling for everyone to settle down or he would have the police board the plane to restore order. Then another voice pierced the crowd.

"Nobody wants to go to Dallas more than I do," the man

declared. "My mother is being buried tomorrow. But there is nothing we can do. Now everyone sit down and let's go."

The passengers immediately quieted down. By his reasoning, the sooner they got back to Germany, the sooner they would be able to find another flight to the United States. The pilot addressed the passengers and said he wouldn't force anyone to go to Germany. And if they wanted to get off the plane now, they could do so.

Beth stood up. She wanted off the plane. She was still shaking and crying. Billy followed her out with Diana. As he walked down the aisle, one of the passengers grabbed his arm. It was a man Billy had spent a lot of time talking to at the Lions Club. He liked him and found him to be a decent fellow.

"I think your family should stay on the plane," he told Billy.

Beth was already at the door and Billy followed her.

Lisa Cox, meanwhile, was still pleading with her mother and sister to get off the plane. They eventually convinced her it was best to stay on board.

The Wakefields were escorted to the same holding area as Clark and Roxanne Loper and Tera and Jason Saarista. Beth was still crying and Billy was visibly upset. None of them had any idea what to expect when the pilot walked in.

"You have two minutes to decide if you are getting on the plane," he said, clearly angry and frustrated. "Then we're leaving whether you come or not."

Roxanne and Clark had already made up their minds, as had Tera and Jason. They were staying put. Beth and Billy, however, were still trying to decide. Billy kept hearing his friend's words on the plane encouraging him to stay.

"I think we should go," he told his wife in a hushed voice.

Beth didn't know what to do. She was terrified that if they went to Europe, it might take them days or even weeks to obtain another flight to the United States. She couldn't bear the thought of being away from her son that much longer. Who knew how long airspace in the United States might be closed to foreign airplanes? If they stayed in Canada, she thought, they could always drive home.

"I'm leaving," the pilot huffed. "Make up your mind right now."

Once again, Billy said he thought they should go.

"Okay," Beth said. They quickly hugged everyone good-bye and followed the pilot back to the plane.

The others watched as the plane taxied away. Roxanne could feel her stomach tighten as the doubts began to creep in. Oh my God, she thought to herself. What have I done? They watched as the plane sped down the runway, became airborne, and then climbed, its lights growing more and more faint in the distance.

No sooner was the plane out of sight than Roxanne felt an amazing sense of relief. All of her doubts were gone. She knew they had made the right decision.

The guard assigned to watch them just shook his head and grimaced. This was the first local person they had encountered during their stay in Gander who didn't smile. Roxanne dubbed him "the meanest Canadian."

∎

Airport and government officials didn't know what to do with the remnants of Lufthansa Flight 438—the Lopers (Roxanne and Clark and their two-year-old daughter, Alexandria) and the Saaristas (Tera and Jason, and their two kids, ten-year-old Colby and four-year-old Kennedy). After refusing to get on the flight back to Germany, the two families were held under guard for more than an hour. Finally, someone in authority realized they didn't have to do anything with them. It was up to the couples to figure out their own way home. And so they were released.

Entering the airport terminal this time, there were no Red Cross tables set up to help them. No CARE packages with sandwiches and water. No school buses waiting outside.

Just moving through the terminal wasn't going to be easy. Since the couples didn't get on the plane, neither did their luggage, which they now had to carry with them. For Roxanne and Clark it wasn't that big a nuisance, only a couple of suitcases. Tera and Jason, however, were a different story. A sergeant in the United States Army, Jason was moving his family back home from Germany, where he had been stationed for three years. He was due to report to warrant-officer school at Fort Rutger in Dotham, Alabama, on September 27, but before he could do that, he had to get his family settled. They had eleven pieces of luggage that they needed to claim, as well as a cat, which the local SPCA had been caring for.

By the time they gathered everything together, the two families looked like the Joad clan in *The Grapes of Wrath.* Tired and angry, with a mountain of belongings, three young children, a cat, and four adults, one of whom was five months pregnant, they stood in the middle of the airport terminal in Gander, Newfoundland trying to figure out how they were going to get to Texas, which on a straight line was 2,423 miles away. No problem, Roxanne thought.

"Hey, Bruce," she said, holding an airport pay phone in one hand and the piece of paper MacLeod had given her in the other. "Guess what? We're still here."

Roxanne ran quickly through the events of the last few hours.

"How many got off?" MacLeod asked.

"There's seven of us," she said. "And a lot of luggage."

"I'll be there in ten minutes with two vans," he said.

Within an hour they were all sitting around the MacLeods'

dinner table trying to determine their next move. A call to various airlines revealed U.S. airspace was still closed down, which only made Roxanne and Clark angrier at Lufthansa. How could they have promised to fly them to Dallas earlier in the day when everything was shut down? The pilot must have deliberately lied to avoid getting into an argument with his passengers.

Since no one knew when flights into the U.S. would resume, the couples decided their best option was to drive home. This seemed a simple enough proposition until they looked at the map. Newfoundland is an island. They would need to drive 330 miles from Gander to the town of Port aux Basques, where they could catch a ferry for a six-hour boat ride to the port city of Sydney in Nova Scotia. From there it was another four hundred miles to the U.S. border in Maine.

Hashing things out that night, they identified three problems.

First, all of the rental cars in town were taken. Second, even if they found a rental car in Canada, they were told they wouldn't be allowed to take it on a one-way trip into the United States, which meant they would have to drive to the border, return their Canadian rental car on the Canadian side of the line, somehow cross into the United States, and then rent another car for the trip to Texas.

Assuming they could work out the first two bugs, they still had a third problem, which they only discovered when they called to find out the ferry schedule in Port aux Basque. After relaying the departure times of the ferry, the operator warned that the service might have to shut down for a few days.

And why was that?

"Well," the ferry operator said, "because of the hurricane."

DAY FOUR

Friday

September 14

CHAPTER SIXTEEN

Gander mayor Claude Elliott and George Vitale.

Roxanne Loper awoke Friday morning feeling lousy. Her throat was sore, her body ached, and her head felt like it was all stuffed up. A registered nurse, she knew she was coming down with the flu, and the timing couldn't be worse. After refusing to get on her Lufthansa flight back to Germany, Roxanne was still trying to figure out the best way to get home.

She and her husband had already overcome their first hurdle—renting a van. With Bruce MacLeod's help, early that morning they found the last available vehicle in Gander, an eight-passenger van complete with a TV and VCR. And they needed a van that size to accommodate Roxanne and her husband, Clark, and their daughter Alexandria, as well as Tera and Jason Saarista and their two kids.

Their next hurdle was the tricky one. Since they couldn't take the rental vehicle across the border, they were going to need help. As Clark, Bruce, and Jason went to pick up the van, Roxanne called her mother back in Texas to see if she had any ideas. Sure enough, she did. And she could sum it up in two words: the Puccis.

While Roxanne and Clark were stranded in Canada, Mike and Leslie Pucci had been calling Roxanne's mother to see if they were okay. Roxanne and Clark knew the Puccis because both couples had used the same agency to adopt their first kids.

When the Puccis learned Roxanne and Clark were trying to find a way across the border, Mike Pucci volunteered the help of his mother, Pat Fletcher, who lives in Stueben, Maine, about fifty miles from the Canadian border. According to the plan, Pat Fletcher and her husband, Frank, would meet the two families in St. John, New Brunswick—the closest Canadian border town where the rented van could be returned—and then drive them into the United States, where they could rent another vehicle for the drive to Texas.

Now all they had to worry about was the hurricane.

Hurricane Erin had started as a tropical wave off the west coast of Africa on August 30. By September 1, it was upgraded to a tropical storm, breaking apart and re-forming several times as it moved lazily across the Atlantic. On the eighth it strengthened into a hurricane, generating winds of 120 mph, making it the first major storm of the hurricane season. Officials at the National Hurricane Center in Miami posted storm warnings for Bermuda and grew concerned that Erin might eventually make landfall in the United States. For the next three days, Erin moved along a straight line, pointing like a dagger toward the northeastern states.

On the morning of September 11, however, it had suddenly turned away from the United States and, like everything else in the air that dreadful day, appeared to be "diverted" to Newfoundland.

By Friday, September 14, the storm had weakened somewhat, but it was still classified as a hurricane, and if it persisted in threatening western Newfoundland, the ferry would have to shut down service until it passed. Roxanne and the others decided to press on; it would take them at least eight hours to drive across the province to the port town where the ferry was located. If the storm turned again, they'd be able to get on the 8 A.M. Saturday ferry, and with any luck, they could cross into the United States some time Sunday.

By the time the van was loaded, the families truly did look like characters out of a Steinbeck novel. There were bags and suitcases strapped onto the roof, while the cat was allowed to roam free inside the van. It was raining when Bruce and Sue MacLeod walked the two families outside for the last time to say good-bye and wish them well. Roxanne didn't know what to say. "Thank you" certainly didn't seem adequate. It had been less than seventy-two hours since they met, and yet so much had occurred. With Jason behind the wheel and Alexandria screaming inside the van because she didn't like being secured in a car seat, Roxanne quickly gave the MacLeods a hug and jumped in. This was going to be one long ride.

❙

Olesya Buntylo could finally relax. The seventeen-year-old Moldovan who was on her way to a new life in the United States had finally reached her family back home in the town of Baltsi, in the northern part of the country. Being able to call home was difficult, and she knew her parents were worried. When she finally got them, they cried over the phone. They had seen the news reports about the planes crashing into the buildings in New York and were certain Olesya had been on one of those flights.

Hearing her mother's voice was a welcome relief for Olesya, who was seven months pregnant with her first child. Starting a new life in a new country was hard enough; doing it pregnant was another matter. And now to be stranded in yet another strange country was all the more unsettling. Olesya refused to complain. She didn't want to seem ungrateful. And by Friday, all of the Moldovan families at the Baptist church in Gander were adapting well to their new surroundings. The younger kids were learning the joys of American culture through an assortment of Woody Woodpecker and Road Runner videos that a local dentist had brought over.

The older kids spent time playing soccer on the grass in front of the church. Clark Piercey brought his two daughters, ages nine and seven, along to play. Other church families brought their kids, too. The language difficulties didn't seem to bother the kids, who acted as if they had been playing together for years. The adults were also finding ways to bond. The women spent time with one another in the kitchen, preparing special meals, while the men played chess and backgammon.

At night they gathered together to sing. Shawn Wiseman, a member of the church and a local musician, would play various gospel songs and hymns on his guitar to see which melodies their guests knew. They were familiar with "Jesus Loves Me," "When the Roll Is Called Up Yonder," and "Silent Night, Holy Night." Of course, the Moldovans knew the words to the songs in Russian and the Baptists sang them in English, which made for an interesting arrangement. With Wiseman on the guitar, back and forth they would sing, one verse in English, the next in Russian.

When they ran out of gospel songs, Wiseman would lead his fellow church members in a few traditional Newfoundland tunes like "Jack Was Every Inch a Sailor" and "Aunt Martha's Sheep." Olesya and the others listened, not really understanding the words, but recognizing the joy in the voices.

❚

After a chaotic night sleeping on the floor of the Hotel Gander ballroom, the passengers of Continental Flight 23 were in a foul mood. They had spent two days in Appleton, where they were treated with warmth and kindness, when they were rounded up shortly before 10 P.M. Thursday and told their flight was cleared to leave and they needed to get to the airport as quickly as possible. They had time only for a few hasty goodbyes before the buses arrived to drive them the eleven miles to the airport.

When they arrived at the terminal, however, they were told there had been a mistake and their plane wasn't taking off. Instead they would be taken to a local hotel—not to check into rooms but to camp out until further notice in the hotel's ballroom. Some passengers asked if they could return to Appleton; they'd been comfortable there, and knew the people. Unfortunately, they were told, that was out of the question.

Twelve hours later the plane's pilot and crew showed up at the hotel to update the passengers. By this point, late Friday morning, they were growing cranky. The pilot, Tom Carroll, apologized for their being needlessly uprooted from Appleton. He said he knew their ultimate destination, Newark

International Airport, was still closed, and wasn't sure why local officials had bothered to bring them to the airport on Thursday.

From an aviation standpoint, Carroll explained, the situation in the United States was constantly changing. Some airports were open, while others were closed. There were new threats and warnings on an hourly basis, and there was no guarantee Newark would open any time in the near future.

"What do you think about going to Houston?" the pilot asked. Houston was Continental's home base, and it appeared that it would open relatively soon.

Passengers became irate. The Europeans on the plane, afraid of flying into the middle of a war in the United States, wanted to return to Dublin. The Americans wanted to press forward, but they weren't keen on flying to Houston. They preferred to wait for Newark, especially since many of them were from the New York City and wanted to get home to be with their families. Arguments erupted among clusters of passengers. One passenger stood and called for a voice vote.

"All those in favor of going back to Dublin, say 'aye'!"

About a third of the room raised their voices.

"All those for going on to Newark."

Two-thirds hollered for Newark. The captain, however, wasn't looking for a vote.

"This is not a democracy," he declared, quieting the crowd. "I'm going to do what's safe for you, the crew, and the plane. And if I can get to Houston, I'm going to go."

That was the end of the discussion. By midafternoon, the buses arrived once again to take them to the airport. George Vitale was happy just to be going, even if it was to Texas. On the plane the mood was light and friendly, as the tension of the argument in the ballroom had faded. Unfortunately, one of the passengers who should have been on the plane was missing, which meant all of the luggage had to be removed from the plane while they searched for the missing passenger's bags. After several hours the plane was finally ready to leave. And there was still more good news. Newark had reopened and their plane was cleared to fly there.

Werner Baldessarini had a change of heart.

The corporate jet of a wealthy Saudi businessman was scheduled to arrive later in the day to pick up the Hugo Boss chairman. Early in the morning, however, Baldessarini picked up the phone and canceled it. He decided he'd rather stay in Gander, at least for now.

It wasn't that the fifty-six-year-old enjoyed sleeping on army cots on the floor of a high school gym with several hundred people. And truth be told, they weren't even cots. They were actually stretchers with four tiny legs that rested about six inches off the ground. But after two days of living with his fellow passengers, he felt an incredible bond with all of them, as if they were part of something special. They slept together. They ate together. They played cards and watched television together.

The bond with the passengers was rivaled only by his attachment to the townspeople, whose compassion was so overwhelming. They took their visitors on driving tours of the countryside. They took them to their homes. The passengers weren't treated like refugees, but like long-lost relatives, and the more he thought about it, the more it moved Baldessarini.

Coming from an environment as cutthroat as the fashion industry, Baldessarini realized this was not a feeling to ignore or casually dismiss. This was something to be relished. And given everything that was going wrong in the world, it was reassuring to see that right now, right here, in one small corner of the planet, something was going right.

There was no hatred. No anger. No fear in Gander. Only the spirit of community. Here, everyone was equal, everyone was treated the same. Here, the basic humanity of man wasn't just surviving but thriving. And Baldessarini understood that he was a witness to it and it was affecting him in ways he'd never imagined.

His assistants in Frankfurt thought he was crazy when he called to cancel the private jet. He tried explaining that flying home while the others were left behind would have been an act of betrayal of everything that had happened over the last seventy-two hours. Wherever his fellow passengers went, that's where he would go. However long it took them to get home, that's how long he'd be gone. He was in this until the end.

❚

During Lufthansa Flight 438's return to Frankfurt, Beth and Billy Wakefield wondered if they had made the right decision. They flew all night Thursday, arriving in Germany Friday morning. After they waited several hours at the airport, an agent for Lufthansa told them he might have good news. He couldn't get them directly home to Nashville, Tennessee, he explained. "But I think I can get you on a flight to Canada," he said. From Canada, the agent explained, they shouldn't have much trouble arranging a flight into the United States.

Beth couldn't believe her ears. Was this some sort of cruel joke? Were there hidden cameras capturing this moment for some sadistic German version of *Bloopers and Practical Jokes*? They had just *come* from Canada. When the ticket agent realized what had happened to the Wakefields, he apologized and excused himself. More than ever, Beth had doubts about their decision. Their little girl, Diana, was cutting two new teeth and nursing an ear infection, so she was still crying all the time. Now it looked like they would just be right back where they started.

Then along came more bad news. They wouldn't be able to get on any flight on Friday. They were going to have to spend the night. Only there weren't any hotel rooms left in the city. They were taken ninety minutes outside of Frankfurt to a cottage in the country. By now the Wakefields had no idea where they were.

Saturday night they finally left Germany, this time for good. They flew from Frankfurt to Chicago and boarded an American Airlines flight for Nashville. They arrived at the Nashville airport at 8 A.M. Sunday morning and were greeted by friends. A few hours later Beth and Billy were reunited with their son, Rob.

▌

Sitting in the faculty lounge of the Lakewood Academy in the town of Glenwood, Rabbi Leivi Sudak believed he'd been brought to this corner of the world for a reason. His trip was supposed to be a one-day journey in which he would fly from London to New York, where he would visit the grave of Rabbi Menachem Mendel Schneerson, the longtime leader of the Lubavitcher movement, who had died in 1994. Once there, he would say his prayers, remembering the names of his family and the people closest to him, and then return to the airport and fly home to England that same night.

In London, Rabbi Sudak spends his working days with disenchanted young people who have taken to the streets and gotten themselves into trouble with drugs and petty crime.

Here in Newfoundland, he realized, there were things for him to learn, especially the lesson that in spite of the tragedies, there are good people in the world. And he was among some of them now.

Baila Hecht felt the same way. The wife of Rabbi Shea Hecht of New York, she happened to be on the same plane with Rabbi Sudak. The two had known each other for many years. Her husband and the rabbi were good friends. Hecht had been traveling home with her thirteen-year-old daughter, Esther, when their flight veered off to Gander.

Most of the people in Gander had had little, if any, contact with someone who was Jewish, and fewer still had ever met an Orthodox Jew. Despite this, the folks in town were not only accepting but genuinely curious. People would regularly come by and ask if it was all right to ask them questions about their beliefs, and both Hecht and Rabbi Sudak enjoyed the discussions that followed.

During one talk with Eithne Smith's husband, Carl, who is a Mountie, the rabbi asked if there was much of a drug problem in Newfoundland. Carl said there was, and added that officials estimated that between 10 and 15 percent of the students in high school had tried marijuana. It was clear to the rabbi, from Carl's voice and demeanor, that he was embarrassed by this figure. In London, the rabbi thought to himself, the number of high school students who had tried marijuana is closer to 80 percent. One reason for the difference was evident to both Hecht and Rabbi Sudak. Looking around the school, they could see a large number of young people from the town working as volunteers alongside their parents. This was the very definition of community for Rabbi Sudak. A community bound by faith and common values. This, too, was one of the lessons Rabbi Sudak believed he was in Newfoundland to be reminded of.

When the call came for them to leave Friday evening, a

new problem surfaced. Three of the seventy-one passengers—Rabbi Sudak, Baila Hecht, and her daughter, Esther—could not travel on the Sabbath. From sundown Friday until sundown Saturday, their faith prevents them not only from traveling, but from engaging in any activity that drew their attention away from their religious observances on the day when God rested after creating the universe, the world, and man. On the Sabbath, Orthodox Jews refrain from riding in a car, cooking meals, watching television, or using any type of machine, including telephones. Even turning on a light switch is prohibited.

As the rest of the passengers from their flight boarded buses for the airport, Rabbi Sudak and the Hechts remained in the school. Two families who lived within walking distance offered to take them in for the night. Rabbi Sudak went with one and the Hechts with the other. More than a test of faith, Rabbi Sudak had a feeling he was meant to stay in Newfoundland for another reason, perhaps another lesson. He just wasn't sure what it might be.

▌

There were 361 passengers aboard American Trans Air Flight 8733, and at least 90 of them were children. ATA is a discount airline favored by travel agents in England who book package tours to the United States. The group on this plane was flying from Manchester, England, to Orlando, Florida. They were going to Disney World.

The thought of so many kids having their hearts broken because their trip to the Magic Kingdom was in jeopardy was distressing for the people in Gander. And when they discovered that at least four of the kids were going to the amusement park to celebrate their birthdays, well, that was more than the folks in town could bear. Town officials and the staff at St. Paul's Intermediate, where the passengers were staying, threw a giant birthday party for all of the children at the school who were turning a year older while they were in Gander.

The local supermarket donated a massive birthday cake— enough to feed four hundred people—while the teachers and students at the school tried to create a miniature Disney World of their own. They decorated the cafeteria with streamers and balloons, and three girls from the local high school volun- teered to dress up in fairy-princess costumes. Replacing Mickey Mouse and Goofy were Commander Gander and the Royal Canadian Mounted Police Safety Bear, two costumed mascots who visit schools in the area telling kids to stay off crack and not to set fires. As their names imply, one is a giant bird and the other is a bear in a Mountie uniform. The kids seemed to love them.

Constable Oz Fudge's seventeen-year-old daughter, Lisa, donned the Commander Gander outfit and was mobbed by kids who wanted to hug her. They sang songs and played games and handed out prizes, and each of the birthday kids received gifts. Nigel Radford couldn't believe the effort everyone in town had made. Radford was traveling with his fiancée, Karen. They were going to be married in Florida. Accompanying them on the trip were ten members of their family who would wit- ness the wedding and spend a week enjoying the different amusement parks—Disney World, Universal Studios, Epcot. The family had saved up two years for this trip.

Radford had his two sons with him, Lewis, who was two, and Cameron, who was five. His brother and his sister were along as well, and they each brought their kids. All the kids had a great time at the party. Some were even upset when it was cut short because word had come in from the airport that their flight was ready to leave. They were going to make it to Disney World after all.

▮

Since Tuesday morning, Corporal Grant Smith had been spending nearly all of his time at the airport, searching bags and checking passports. Normally, the twenty-six-year veteran of the RCMP was assigned to the region's drug task force. Over the years smugglers prodding for entry points into North America had found their way to Gander. In recent months the Mounties had seized a ton of cocaine in one bust and almost twenty-six tons of hashish in another.

Smith was in his office, just down the road from the airport, when he heard about the attacks on New York and the planes, which were already beginning to circle Gander on their final approach before landing. He was ordered to help with security at the airport. Tensions had run high during those first twenty-four hours as Smith and his fellow Mounties scrutinized passengers looking for additional terrorists.

Three days later, as more and more passengers were preparing to leave Gander, Smith was still concerned about terrorists, but he also wanted to do something special for the town's unexpected guests. He felt a deep sense of pride in the way the people in Gander and the surrounding communities had responded to this tragedy. And he was equally proud of the passengers, for being so well behaved and understanding. Everyone remained calm and levelheaded. There wasn't a single arrest during the entire week.

Smith was determined that the stranded passengers' last memory of Gander would be a positive one. Security for each of the outgoing flights was unprecedented, with passengers having to clear two and sometimes three checkpoints. The lines were long and the wait could seem interminable. Some passengers were visibly nervous about getting on a plane again. Smith encouraged his fellow Mounties to find ways to ease their fears and not make the screening process needlessly bureaucratic and impersonal. Smith led the charge.

"Your passport and a smile," he would say when a passenger walked up to his station. If they responded with a confused look, he'd tell them, "You can't leave Canada without a passport and a smile."

His wife was a volunteer at Gander Academy, where she was also a teacher. At night she would tell him stories about the plane people she'd met. On at least a dozen occasions over the ensuring days, Smith drew from this knowledge while reviewing passports and stunned departing passengers by recalling their names and some small detail about them.

To one couple he remarked: "Oh, you're the one who ate all the fish at Noonan's house." And to another: "I believe Betty Smith was taking care of you in town."

For most people, this was their first encounter with a Mountie, and it certainly wasn't what they expected. For one thing, they were dressed like ordinary police officers. This was a letdown for those folks whose images of Mounties were rooted in decades of movies, television shows, and cartoons. Nelson Eddy singing to Jeanette MacDonald in *Rose Marie*. Shirley Temple as a darling waif who survives an Indian massacre in *Susannah of the Mounties*. The classic fifties TV show *Sergeant Preston of the Yukon* and its dismal nineties counterpart, *Due South*. And, of course, there was the animated genius of Dudley Do-Right.

The common ingredient in all of these memories—apart from the promise that "the Mounties always get their man"— was the clothing, the ubiquitous red tunic and broad-brimmed hat. Neither of which Smith and his cohorts were wearing. Smith could sense his appearance was an area of disappointment for passengers, some of whom would plaintively ask, "Where's your hat?"

Determined to turn things around, Smith received permission from his superiors to wear the RCMP dress uniform to the airport on Friday and Saturday. The formal attire, known as the Red Serge, is an eye-catching ensemble, usually reserved for ceremonial occasions. It consists of high brown leather boots with a matching belt, a rakish leather strap cutting across the chest from the left shoulder to the right hip, three-inch-long spurs, navy-blue riding pants with thick yellow stripes down the side, a Stetson with a wide, flat brim, and the scarlet coat with gold buttons, a navy-blue collar, and navy-blue epaulets.

For those two days, all eyes were on Smith when he strode through the airport. Like paparazzi catching a glimpse of Madonna, passengers ran to snap his picture. In turn, he demanded that they pose alongside him for the next shot. Eagerly they complied. Some stood rigidly next to him. Others embraced him. Smith's expression, though, was always the same, his greenish-brown eyes twinkling under that massive hat, his thick blond mustache curled above a proud smile, his five-foot eight-inch frame standing a bit taller.

And so it went, one after another. *Click. Click. Click.* His picture, and all the warmth and good spirit it represented, captured on film by hundreds of passengers, a final memento of this life-altering detour.

❙

For her entire life, Hannah O'Rourke has been deathly afraid of water, to the point where she wouldn't even go to the beach, stand in the surf, and let the ocean rise up to her ankles. Her kids always assumed it had something to do with her journey to America as an Irish immigrant. She'd come to this country by boat almost fifty years before and never set foot on one again. All of which presented a problem for her family, since Hannah was currently trapped on an island.

One of her son's best friends—Maryann's brother—was prepared to drive into Canada to pick Hannah and Dennis up if it looked like they were going to be stuck there much longer. If Hannah and Dennis could get to the ferry in Port aux Basque and cross over to Nova Scotia, he would meet them there and drive them home. The trip was about a thousand miles each way. Maryann decided to see if Hannah would be interested.

"Gran, there's a ferry that goes over to Nova Scotia," she said. "We could pick you up there and bring you home. Would you be willing to get on the ferry?"

"Yes," Hannah said without hesitation. "If I have to swim to get home, that's what I'll do."

Maryann was stunned. When she told the others Hannah's response, they, too, were amazed. "Wow," Patricia said, "she really must want to get out of there."

In the end, the ferry ride wasn't necessary when they discovered that their plane, Aer Lingus Flight 105, would be able to take off that afternoon. Before Hannah and Dennis left, they were visited by a delegation from the Gander Volunteer Fire Department. The chief of the department had just learned the O'Rourkes' son was a missing New York firefighter and he wanted to pay his respects and let them know that if there was anything anyone in his department could do for them, all they had to do was ask.

Saying good-bye to Hannah and Dennis was difficult for their new friends at the legion hall. Beulah Cooper told them she would keep praying for Kevin, as did the others at the legion hall—Wally Crummel, Alf Johnson, and his wife, Karen. Even Tom Mercer, when he heard the O'Rourkes' flight was ready to leave, raced over to the hall to say good-bye. He gave them each a hug and wished them well.

Neither Hannah nor Dennis knew how to express how

much all of these people had meant to them during this horrendous time. When they arrived in Gander, it had been unbearable to be so far away from the love and support of their family. Now it felt to them like they, in fact, had a family in Gander.

The flight to Dublin was uneventful. Between the steady stream of phone calls from the O'Rourke family and a few pointed inquiries from Hillary Clinton's office, Aer Lingus officials were not going to take any chances with Hannah and Dennis O'Rourke. When their plane landed in Dublin at 2:30 A.M., they were met by four agents for the airline, who escorted them through the airport and guaranteed them they would be on the next possible flight to New York.

Hannah's brothers and sisters in Ireland also met the plane. Only a few days before they had all been together under happier circumstances. Hannah had had no idea she would see them again so soon, and the reason crippled her with anguish. Not even the sight of her siblings could allay her fears. The next available plane to New York was set to leave in ten hours. She still wondered if her family on Long Island was hiding the truth from her. Did they already know Kevin was dead? Had they found his body? Were they waiting to tell her in person? Ten more hours and another plane trip across the ocean and she would be home, and then she'd know the answer.

CHAPTER SEVENTEEN

Karaoke at the Trailways Pub.

The most infamous of Newfoundland traditions is the "Screeching-In" ceremony, which allows a visitor to become an honorary Newfie through a series of challenges that test the strength of person's stomach, the deftness of his or her tongue, and his or her ability to drink an unhealthy amount of alcohol. Not just any alcohol. One must drink a brand of liquor unique to Newfoundland. A lowbrow rum known affectionately as Screech.

The history of Screech has long been debated in Newfoundland. In the 1970s, the Canadian government issued its
own official account.

> *Long before any liquor board was created to take alcohol
> under its benevolent wing, Jamaican rum was the main-
> stay of the Newfoundland diet, with salt fish traded to the
> West Indies in exchange for rum. When the Government
> took control of the traditional liquor business in the early
> 20th century, it began selling the rum in an unlabelled
> bottle. The product might have remained permanently
> nameless except for the influx of American servicemen to
> the island during World War II. As the story goes, the com-
> manding officer of the original detachment was having
> his first taste of Newfoundland hospitality and, imitating
> the custom of his host, downed his drink in one gulp. The
> American's blood-curdling howl, when he regained his
> breath, brought the sympathetic and curious from miles
> around rushing to the house to find what was going on.
> The first to arrive was a garrulous old American sergeant
> who pounded on the door and demanded, "What the
> cripes was that ungodly screech?" The taciturn New-
> foundlander who had answered the door replied simply,
> "The Screech? 'Tis the rum, me son." Thus was born a leg-
> end. As word of the incident spread, the soldiers, deter-
> mined to try this mysterious "Screech" and finding its
> effects as devastating as the name implies, adopted it as
> their favorite.*

According to author, Professor Pat Byrne, a longtime
scholar on Newfoundland traditions at Memorial University in
St. John's, the Screeching-In ceremony itself can be an elaborate affair in which the person being initiated stands before

the chief Screecher, dressed in traditional Newfoundland fishing garb, which to outsiders can best be described as the yellow outfit worn by the fellow on a box of Gorton's frozen fish sticks. The initiate is given a few Newfoundland delicacies to eat, such as "Newfie steak," known elsewhere around the world as bologna. The person is even asked to kiss a freshly caught cod as a sign of respect toward the importance of the fish in the economy of Newfoundland. This is followed by a series of questions the Screecher asks, in a heightened accent, which in turn is supposed to elicit a set response from the initiate.

SCREECHER: Is we Newfies?

INITIATE: Deed we is, me old cock, an' long may yer big jib draw.

SCREECHER: Did ye j'st go down on yer knucks and kiss a smelly old codfish?

INITIATE: Deed we did, me old cock.

SCREECHER: Did ye j'st wrap yer chops around a piece of Newfie steak and gobble some dried caplin?

INITIATE: Deed we did, me old cock.

As Professor Byrne points out, this question-and-answer period can go on for as long as the master of ceremonies wants to ask questions.

SCREECHER: Did ye all j'st repeat a whole lot o'tings ye don't un'erstand a-tall?

INITIATE: Deed we did, me old cock.

Once the last question is answered, the person is given a large shot of Screech to down in a single gulp, to the applause and cheers of those around them. An actual certificate is even presented, bearing witness to the event and making the person an honorary Newfoundlander.

In the days following September 11, hundreds, if not thousands, of stranded passengers went through some variation of the Screeching-In ceremony across the island. Usually it wasn't as elaborate or as time-consuming as an official ceremony. But in every town, from Stephenville in the west to St. John's in the east, a Screecher held a rotting cod in his hands and had people line up to kiss it. It was the natives' good-natured way of sharing a little bit of their past with their guests. Nowhere was that enthusiasm greater than in Gambo at the Trailways Pub. By some estimates, more than 150 of the 900 passengers were Screeched-In over a two-day period.

Without question, the Trailways was the most popular spot in Gambo during these days. Every night the passengers came in and drank the place dry. And every day the owners sent one of their bartenders twenty minutes down the road to Glovertown to load up on supplies to restock their coolers. Over three nights they went through more than two hundred cases of beer, more kegs than they could count, and enough hard liquor to embalm a herd of moose.

By Friday night the bar was so full that people were spilling out through the back door. After spending a quiet Thursday evening at George and Edna Neal's home, the gang—Deb Farrar, Winnie House, Lana Etherington, Bill Cash, Mark Cohen, and their newest member, Greg Curtis—decided to let loose with a final night at the pub. They all felt there was a good chance they would be leaving on Saturday and so this was probably their last night together.

When word reached some of the locals that Winnie was a Nigerian princess, the daughter of an African chieftain, they knew they needed to bestow their highest honor on her. She needed to be Screeched-In. By this time in the evening,

Winnie had already been drinking a fair amount of wine and was up for anything.

Jim Lane, a volunteer firefighter, was the designated Screecher in Gambo, and for the past two nights he'd been a busy man. Passengers were eager to be Screeched-In and Lane was glad to oblige. Dressed in the traditional yellow oilskin and sporting a most unkempt and dirty phony white beard, he created a mini-ceremony that may have been short on tradition but was long on enjoyment. Also making an appearance on Friday was the same rotting codfish he'd been using all week. Time was not kind to this fish and Lane had to hold the slimy cod carefully to keep its guts from spilling out.

Lane was honored when he learned that Winnie was interested. He did his best to explain the ceremony to her, but her attention span at that moment was somewhat limited. He recited her one line—"Deed we is, me old cock, an' long may yer big jib draw"—and asked her to repeat it for practice. Winnie squealed with laughter.

Lane warned her not to laugh when he asked her the official question.

"Are you ready, me dear?" Lane asked.

"Yes," Winnie said, trying to straighten herself up.

"Okay," he said, falling into character. "Is we Newfies?"

"Deed . . . me cock . . ." Winnie said, bursting into fits of laughter.

Every time she made a mistake they had her drink another shot of Screech. And while such penalties aren't an actual part of the regular ceremony, in this case it was plain fun.

"Is we Newfies?"

"Deed we . . ." she said, followed by more laughing.

Finally, after two or three times, she came close enough for Lane to accept it. After all, he didn't want her to get too drunk.

"Now kiss the cod," he told her, holding the five-pounder to her face.

"I can't kiss that." Winnie shuddered.

"Ah, but you must kiss the cod," Lane explained.

In unison, those around them began chanting, "Kiss the cod! Kiss the cod!"

"I can't, I can't," she squealed, her voice so high it could attract wolves.

Lane moved the fish closer to her face.

"I can't, I can't," she said, closing her eyes.

Lane didn't know what to do. If she didn't kiss the cod, he couldn't give her the Screecher certificate. And after she had come all this way, he didn't want to see her fail. Then it dawned on him. He'd have to give her a little help.

Ever so gently, he flicked his wrist and thwapped her on the mouth with the head of the fish.

"Eeewwww!" she screamed.

But it was over, she'd have her certificate, and everyone cheered.

❚

The second half of the evening was marked by the introduction of a karaoke machine. People were more than eager to sing, and onstage the karaoke went nonstop. To describe the singing as awful would be charitable, but then again, the purpose of these machines is for people to become entertaining at the expense of the song. There was hope, however. The Beatle Boys were in the house.

Since she'd first met them on the flight, Jessica Naish wanted to hear them sing. Having spent three days with them only made her more curious. Peter Ferris, who assumed the role of George Harrison in the band, was willing to get up and sing for the crowd. But Paul Moroney, the John Lennon of the group, was against it, which in a way should have been expected, since Lennon was always the moodiest of the Beatles.

Naish kept nagging for Moroney to play and encouraged others in the pub to do the same. Her Yoko-like behavior eventually paid off. It wasn't that Moroney was trying to be difficult; he was afraid of sounding bad since his voice wasn't well rested. Moroney and Ferris whispered for a few moments, trying to decide what song was appropriate. Finally, Moroney walked over to the karaoke machine by himself. A few people closest to the stage area quieted down.

"This is a song by John Lennon," Moroney said, without any other comments. As the music came up, he stepped to the microphone.

Moroney's fears were unfounded. He was in fine voice. More important, his tone, his styling, matched Lennon's perfectly. Naturally, having a pretty liquored-up crowd didn't hurt either. Standing off to one side of the room, Ferris watched as more and more people in the bar stopped what they were doing and turned their attention to Moroney.

As he moved into the second verse of "Imagine," the bar was largely silent, with all eyes on Moroney. A few people mouthed the words along with him as he sang. Most just watched and swayed. Given the events of the last seventy-two hours, Ferris knew the lyrics had taken on a special meaning; the hope of being able to live life in peace. And seeing the expressions of those around him made it clear that he wasn't alone. He even noticed a few people becoming teary-eyed. In all his years of performing with the group, Ferris had never seen people react so emotionally.

As the song came to its conclusion, the last notes hung in the air for a few seconds and the pub was still. Then all at once people were clapping and cheering and hollering for more. Moroney tried to walk offstage, but several people pushed him back. There was no room for debate.

Ferris joined him onstage and they quickly settled on a few more songs. Since the pub was packed with their fellow passengers from Continental Flight 5, they decided "A Hard Day's Night" was appropriate to commemorate the thirty hours they'd all spent together on the plane. From there they segued into "Eight Days a Week"—a prediction as to how long they would probably be stranded in Gambo. Ending on an optimistic note, they sang "We Can Work It Out."

Each song had everyone dancing and singing and carrying on as if it were the actual Beatles. The room was hot and sweaty. Onstage Ferris imagined this must have been what the Liverpool pub the Cavern was like back in 1961 when the real Beatles had played there.

Nobody was happier than Naish. She bopped along to the music, screaming like a teenager seeing the Fab Four for the first time on *The Ed Sullivan Show*. After extolling their talents to everyone all night—without ever having heard them sing— she felt inextricably linked to them. Just before Moroney had gone on, Naish was hit with the thought: What if they aren't any good?

She needn't have worried. They were boffo.

For the rest of the night, they weren't Paul Moroney and Peter Ferris, or even their alter egos, George Harrison and John Lennon. They were the Beatle Boys. Everyone called them the Beatle Boys. The Newfies, of course, said it so fast it sounded like one word—theBeatleBoys. Long after they left town, locals would remember them as theBeatleBoys. As in: "Ay, buddy, you should have been here the night of theBeatle-Boys."

Actually, they could make it seem even more compact. Pronounced as fast as humanly possible, it sounded more like "daBeedaBys." All night long Friday, the cry went out: "Another round for daBeedaBys."

"And don't forget the princess!"

"Ay, that's right, another round for the lovely princess."

The Beatles, a Nigerian princess, and a ripe old cod. Ay, this would indeed be a night they would long remember.

DAYS FIVE AND SIX

Saturday and

Sunday

September 15 and 16

CHAPTER EIGHTEEN

Saturday

Moldovan families leaving the Baptist church.

After driving all night, Roxanne and Clark Loper and Tera and Jason Saarista arrived with their children in Port aux Basques, around 3 A.M. on Saturday. They checked into a pair of motel rooms for a couple of hours' sleep and made it to the dock in time to catch the 8 A.M. ferry.

Overnight, Hurricane Erin had made one last turn and was heading out to sea. By morning it was clear that the storm would only graze the eastern tip of Newfoundland, leaving the ferry open for business. The residual effects of the storm, however, made for a rough ride. The ferry pitched and swayed in the choppy waters between Newfoundland and Nova Scotia. Tera, who was five months pregnant, spent most of the six-hour voyage throwing up. And in the cafeteria, the children had to hold on to their trays while they ate to keep them from sliding off the table.

The flu symptoms Roxanne had been feeling the day before were only getting worse, and once they landed in Sydney, Nova Scotia, they still had a long drive to the U.S. border. At Roxanne's insistence, they ventured along the scenic Highway 6, which winds along Nova Scotia's north shore and would give them a chance to glimpse Prince Edward Island from across the Northumberland Strait.

Ever since reading Lucy Maud Montgomery's *Anne of Green Gables*, Roxanne had wanted to visit Prince Edward Island. The international bestseller, about a plucky orphan and her adventures living on the island, described in loving detail the beauty of the land and the people. The book, and its subsequent sequels, had touched Roxanne, and now that she was with her own adopted daughter, she didn't want to pass up the opportunity to spy Prince Edward Island, even if it was from across the strait.

Saturday night they stopped in the New Brunswick town of St. John, checking into a sleazy motel near the airport, where they'd return the rental van. They were now just fifty miles from the border.

▮

Get up! You're going home!" Barry Bragg was pounding on doors throughout his house, trying to wake his guests, Peter

Ferris, Jessica Naish, and Paul Moroney. When the Trailways Pub had finally closed, the three went back to the Bragg home. Everyone was still excited from the night at the pub, and when the Braggs produced a couple of guitars, they all ended up singing songs until it was light outside.

They had been asleep only a couple of hours when the call came to the Bragg house that Continental Flight 5 had been cleared to go. The three of them had to get to the church immediately, as the buses were ready to leave for the airport.

Deb Farrar, Lana Etherington, Winnie House, Bill Cash, and Mark Cohen were already at the church waiting. They were all feeling a bit groggy. It was definitely time for this unanticipated vacation to come to an end, especially after the wild night at the pub. They had hoped to make a big spaghetti dinner that night at George and Edna Neal's house, but when the call came to report to the church, they put the food away.

As the buses waited for Naish and the Beatle Boys to arrive, Deb and Greg, who was on Delta Flight 117, said their goodbyes. They had struck up a convenient romance during their days in Gambo, spending almost all of their time together. Neither, however, was sure whether it would continue when they got back to the States. Deb lived in Texas, Greg in North Carolina. Their whole time together felt like an episode of one of those shows on MTV—*The Real World* or *Road Rules*—where a whole gamut of feelings, emotions, and experiences are compressed into a frenzied period. They would need a little space and perspective to make sense of it all.

If nothing else, their time together had been a welcome relief from having to think about what was happening back home. They traded phone numbers and addresses. They kissed farewell and off Deb and the others went. In a few hours Continental Flight 5 would be back in Houston, and by Monday, Deb would be back at her job.

▐

Something was definitely wrong with Ralph, the purebred cocker spaniel puppy on his way from Germany to Dallas. Bonnie Harris saw it and so did Linda Humby when they came by Saturday morning to take care of the animals that were still waiting for flights home. The little guy wasn't hungry. He had trouble standing and he appeared listless. Not wanting to take any chances, they called Doc Tweedie.

Examining Ralph for himself, the vet noticed that the pup's hind legs were sensitive and he appeared to be in pain. Tweedie wanted to run a full battery of tests, something he couldn't do at the hangar. He needed to take Ralph to his clinic. He knew, though, that the dog wasn't allowed outside of the hangar, much less off the grounds of the airport.

With the finesse of a cat burglar, Tweedie stashed Ralph in his car and smuggled him out of the airport. After going over him from nose to tail at his clinic and taking X rays of his hindquarters, the vet could find nothing seriously wrong. He was just sore and a little bruised, as if he'd fallen or been accidentally dropped. Tweedie, Harris, and Humby eventually figured out what was happening. It seemed that Ralph's popularity hadn't been limited to the daytime. Employees from the graveyard shift at the airport also loved playing with the puppy, keeping him up all night and letting him run around outside of his cage as much as he wanted.

Ralph wasn't hurt. He was simply exhausted. All he needed was some rest. Harris and Humby put out the word around the airport: no more keeping Ralph up all night. He was a growing dog and he needed his sleep.

The buses arrived at the Baptist church about 7 P.M. to take Olesya Buntylo and the other Moldovan families to the airport for Delta Flight 141. Olesya cried as she said good-bye to Clark Piercey, who had been with them every day since they arrived. As far as the Moldovans were concerned, Piercey was a part of their family now. And leaving him behind was every bit as painful as it had been to leave family members behind in Eastern Europe. When the buses pulled away from the church, Olesya watched all of the Baptists waving good-bye. God will bless them for everything they have done, she thought to herself.

Delta Flight 141 was originally scheduled to fly from Amsterdam to New York and land at Kennedy International Airport on September 11. Now, however, rather than having it fly to New York, Delta officials decided the plane should fly to their home base in Atlanta. When the thirty-eight Moldovans arrived at the airport, they discovered their entry papers into the United States allowed them to come into the country only through New York. Canadian immigration officials told them they would have to remain in Canada for the time being, or risk being detained at a U.S. Immigration and Naturalization detention center in Atlanta while their paperwork was investigated. The Moldovans decided to stay in Gander.

Late that night, Piercey received a phone call from Olesya telling him that she and the others were still in Gander. Immigration officials were taking them to the Sinbad Hotel until they could arrange a flight to New York. Piercey was sorry their trip had been delayed, but he was also glad to have a chance to see them all again. In the morning he went down to the hotel to make sure they were okay. He kept them company. Helped them get around town. And checked in on them every day until new flights could be arranged, just like any good member of the family.

▍

Hannah and Dennis O'Rourke left Dublin early Saturday afternoon. They weren't on the first plane out, as promised, but they did make it onto the second. When their plane landed in New York, their children Patricia O'Keefe and Dennis O'Rourke were waiting to pick them up. Hannah rushed toward them. After all those hours on the plane, she thought they might have new information about Kevin. And if her fears were right, and the family was holding back information from her, they would tell her now. "There's still no news, Ma," Patricia told her.

At least there was still hope, Hannah thought. They drove to Kevin's home in Hewlett, Long Island, and as the car pulled into the driveway, everyone inside the house came spilling out, including Kevin's wife, Maryann. Everyone was crying and hugging and holding on to each other. After the horrors of the past week, Hannah and Dennis's return home gave everyone a chance to release some of their bottled-up emotions. Now, whatever happened, they would face it together. And they would get through it as a family.

▍

Rabbi Sudak returned to Lakewood Academy on Saturday. By now the passengers from the last plane in Glenwood were on their way to the airport. Since the Rabbi Sudak and Baila

Hecht and her daughter, Esther, felt comfortable at the school, Lakewood officials decided to keep the shelter open on Saturday, even if it was just for three people.

For the first time in days the school was quiet. Eithne Smith, the teacher who had helped arrange to have kosher meals brought to the school back on Wednesday, was sitting with Rabbi Sudak in the school office when the fax machine started to hum. Smith retrieved the message. It was from one of the passengers, Werner Kolb, an alumni of Northwest Flight 61, originally scheduled to fly directly from Amsterdam to New York. Kolb had just made it home to the Netherlands and decided to send a note of thanks to everyone at the school for taking care of him.

"It is not possible for me to tell you how I felt during my stay with you," he wrote. "Only once was I treated in a similar way. This was when I was a child. I was liberated in Holland in 1945. You wonderful Canadians have not changed."

Smith could feel her hands shake as she read the note. After four long days, she was exhausted, and Kolb's note filled her with emotion. She started to cry and Rabbi Sudak spoke to her in comforting tones. He told her that the generosity she and others at the school had showed would be remembered and celebrated for a very long time. Their actions were more than just taking in passengers whose flights had been delayed. The Newfoundlanders had provided a caring haven for hundreds of people at a moment when they were scared and far from home. They were made to feel safe and secure when the world around them seemed anything but.

Smith wanted to hug him, to place her arms around him and squeeze and share his strength, but she remembered that this was forbidden, so she just thanked him.

In the afternoon, a man from Gander came to visit the rabbi. He was at least seventy years old and partially blind from cataracts. He moved stiffly and his health was poor. His name was Eddie Brake.

Although he had lived in Gander for forty years and was a well-known salesman around town, very few people knew he was Jewish. It was a secret he'd kept for a very long time. Even his wife, whom he had been married to for forty-five years, discovered his true religious faith only ten years before when he finally broke down and told her. They had raised seven children, all Catholic like their mother.

The person now known as Ed Brake had been born in Poland in 1929 or 1930, he wasn't sure which. He didn't know the name his parents gave him at birth or, for that matter, his family name. He knew only they were Jewish, and prior to the start of World War II, they had paid to have him smuggled out of Poland and taken to England. Before leaving, Brake remembered being attacked and beaten, and his family living under a constant threat of abuse because they were Jewish.

When he left Poland he was only seven or eight years old. He was adopted by a family in England who moved to Newfoundland in 1936. He grew up in Corner Brook, a bay town on the western edge of the island, and was told never to tell anyone that his birth parents were Jews. Any time he asked questions about being Jewish, his stepparents became enraged, even violent toward him. And so began his secret life as a Jew.

The appearance of Rabbi Sudak stirred up old feelings for Brake. After arriving at Lakewood Academy on Wednesday, the rabbi had asked if there were any Jews in the area, and if so, he would like to meet them. Although hardly anyone knew of Brake's past, one of the people visiting the rabbi told him a little about Brake. The rabbi was eager to meet him.

Brake was scared when he was called and told about the rabbi's wish. He knew his family didn't like it when he discussed his past, and they were still somewhat resentful that he had hidden so much from them for so long. Brake, however, felt the need to go. "It's time," he said to himself. Since he'd come to Newfoundland as a boy in 1936, he has never entered a synagogue or spoken to a rabbi.

On the way to Lakewood, he thought about what he would say and how much he would share. Inside the faculty lounge, sitting around a table with the rabbi and Baila Hecht and a few teachers, he found it all came spilling out. Although he wasn't certain, he believed his parents and his siblings had been rounded up by the Nazis after the invasion of Poland and taken to the camps, where they died. Brake lowered his head and asked the rabbi to pass his fingers over the back of his skull. The rabbi could feel the dents and depressions Brake said were the result of beatings he suffered at the hands of the police in Poland before his parents sent him away. He had other reminders as well, scars on his back and on his feet. He took off his shoes so the rabbi could see.

Brake told about coming to Newfoundland and being raised in a home where it wasn't permitted to talk about Judaism, a fear that stayed with him throughout his adult life. If his stepparents reacted so violently to his being Jewish, how would others respond if they knew? He decided it was best never to tell anyone about his past. Ten years ago he told his wife and his children, he explained, because he couldn't hold it in any longer.

Despite keeping it a secret, Brake told the rabbi he never stopped thinking of himself as a Jew. He showed the rabbi his walking stick. On the handle was engraved a tiny Star of David. Some nights he would wake up at three in the morning, having just dreamed of the religious music he'd heard as a child in Poland. A few days ago, he added, his mother came to him in a dream.

Brake remained stoic, almost detached, as he recounted the story of his life. He was glad the rabbi had sent for him, though. He had wanted someone like the rabbi to hear what he had to say so his story would not be lost when he died. Both Rabbi Sudak and Baila Hecht were moved by Brake's words. They told him he should tell his story to more people. They encouraged him to visit schools, like the one they were in now, and to talk to the children about the Holocaust and about anti-Semitism. With so few Jews in Newfoundland, they argued, it was vital for him to come forward and provide a living example to refute those who denied that such events as the Holocaust had ever taken place.

Brake listened to their pleas. His family, though, didn't want him speaking out. They wanted him to leave the past alone. Brake wasn't one to call attention to himself, anyway, he said. "I'm a secretive person," he explained. But he'd needed to tell someone. And now that he'd told the rabbi, he felt a weight lift off him. After almost two hours, it was time for Brake to get home to his wife. He thanked the rabbi and Hecht for listening, picked up his cane with the tiny Star of David, and slowly shuffled out the door.

And with his departure, Rabbi Sudak stopped wondering why he had he been brought to Newfoundland.

CHAPTER NINETEEN

Sunday

Roxanne Loper heard a knock at her door and opened it to find Pat and Frank Fletcher outside with a van. They'd driven up from Steuben, Maine, that morning to carry the Lopers and the Saaristas across the border. Roxanne felt guilty because the Fletchers had cut short their vacation in order to help them.

They would all cross the border into the United States at a small town on the St. Croix River called Calais. It took a little more than an hour to get there, and the line of cars waiting to cross stretched more than two hundred yards. For Roxanne and Clark, the border was significant for two reasons. First, it meant they were home. The attacks on America had made them anxious to be within its borders again. For the past few days they'd noticed Canadians flying American flags at half-mast in honor of those who had died. They believed the best way they could show support for their own country was to stand proud within it.

The second reason the border was significant was Alexandria. As soon as their adopted baby girl set foot in the United States, her legal status as an American was secure and she would be instantly designated a lawful permanent resident and a United States citizen.

As the line of cars moved slowly toward the checkpoint, Clark decided to walk Alexandria across the bridge and into the United States. Wanting to capture the symbolic moment, he yelled for Roxanne to grab their camcorder. Halfway over the St. Croix River he found a line marking the border. Clark set Alexandria down so one of her feet was on the Canadian side of the line and the other was on the American side. He told Alexandria to wave to Roxanne.

"Alex becomes a citizen the hard way," Roxanne declared. "You had to walk and take boats and fly and drive and your country was attacked."

On the American side of the river, they turned over a large envelope to immigration officials. The sealed envelope had been given to them at the U.S. embassy in Moscow and contained all of Alexandria's paperwork. By the time Alexandria was done being processed, the others were just making it across the border. From there, the Fletchers drove them another ninety miles to Bangor, Maine, the closest town with a car-rental agency open on a Sunday. The Lopers rented a car, the Saaristas a minivan. And once the two families were set, the Fletchers wished them well and returned to the vacation they had interrupted to carry them into the United States.

Since they were headed in the same direction, the two couples followed each other down Interstate 95. Driving through Boston, Roxanne took out her video camera and photographed the signs for Logan International Airport. Clark provided the running commentary, noting how the two planes that struck the World Trade Center had flown out of Logan. Their drive home had turned into an unintended tour of the sites involved in the terrorist attacks.

Taking turns behind the wheel, they drove through the night, and as they approached New York City, they encountered a series of detours designed to keep people away from where a massive rescue effort was still under way around the clock. They reached Washington, D.C., late Monday morning, and stopped that night in Tennessee. One more long day of driving and they'd be home.

❚

In Gander, only a handful of planes were still waiting to leave. Eithne Smith and her husband, Carl, were hoping they could arrange for one of the planes, particularly one of the flights headed for New York, to take Rabbi Sudak and the Hechts. In the morning they drove to the airport, and Carl, being a Mountie, was able to go down on the tarmac to speak directly to the captains of the remaining planes. As Eithne and the others waited in the terminal, Carl pleaded his case to the pilots.

One pilot initially agreed to take them, but at the last minute was ordered by his company not to allow additional passengers on his plane. All of the airlines were fanatical about security and would allow only a plane's original passengers to board.

After several hours wasted at the airport, the group returned to the Smith home to decide what to do next.

The timing for traveling home was tricky because they were approaching Rosh Hashanah, a two-day holiday that marks the start of the Jewish New Year. As with the Sabbath, they weren't allowed to travel. Rosh Hashanah would begun at sundown on Monday, so if they didn't leave in the next twenty-four hours, they would have to stay in Newfoundland until Thursday.

Both Eithne and Carl Smith were perfectly willing to host Rabbi Sudak and the Hechts until Thursday. They even made contingency plans to create a special Rosh Hashanah celebration using the local Lions Club and inviting people from town to participate. But they also knew it was important for the rabbi and the Hechts to be with their families and with others of their faith at such a holy time.

Regular airline service was slowly starting to come alive again on the island, but there weren't any Air Canada flights leaving from Gander in time. Calling around, however, Carl discovered a commercial flight leaving from the town of Stephenville early Monday morning, which would arrive in Halifax in time for a connecting flight to New York. If everything went as planned, Rabbi Sudak and the Hechts would land in New York by mid-afternoon, long before sundown.

All they had to do was get to Stephenville, which was five hours away by car. Without hesitation, Carl and Eithne offered to drive them. Rabbi Sudak was relieved. It would have been impossible for him to rent a car and drive—for two reasons. First, no rental cars were available in Gander. And second, the strict rules of his faith did not allow him to be unchaperoned in a car with a woman who was not his wife.

Before heading out, they all had supper and enjoyed the last of the kosher food that had been prepared. Carl then gave the rabbi a parting gift—one of the large, flat-brimmed Stetsons that the Mounties wear. The rabbi was moved. He certainly didn't have a hat like this at home in London. Later he pulled Eithne aside privately.

"Please teach me how to wear this hat correctly," he asked. "Does this strap go under my chin or behind my head?"

They both laughed at the question, and Eithne explained that the strap was worn across the back of the head to keep the Stetson from falling off.

"I would have been mortified," the rabbi said, thanking her, "if I had worn it wrong and embarrassed Carl."

A little before 9 P.M., Carl and Eithne Smith, Rabbi Sudak, and Baila and Esther Hecht set off on the Trans Canada Highway in the Smiths' minivan. The drive gave Carl and Rabbi Sudak a chance to talk at length. Eithne was amused by the rabbi's ability to weave stories and lessons out of almost any subject. This fellow certainly touched the blarney stone, Eithne thought to herself.

Arriving in Stephenville at 2 A.M., they checked into the Holiday Inn just down the road from the airport. In the lobby, Rabbi Sudak asked Eithne if she would write down the names of her relatives, along with the names of her and Carl's mothers, so he could pray for them, along with the members of his own family, when he visited the grave of the rebbe, Rabbi Schneerson. Before leaving Gander, he had gathered from Lakewood's principal, Jamey Jennings, the names of his family members. Eithne found some paper at the front desk and wrote out a list of names and then everyone said their goodbyes.

In the morning, the rabbi and the Hechts would take a cab to the airport and get on their flight to Halifax. They would arrive in New York in plenty of time to celebrate Rosh Hashanah. Carl and Esther, meanwhile, slept in late at the hotel before driving back to Gander. Even after years of marriage, they had every intention of taking full advantage of a nice hotel room away from the kids.

∎

Sure enough, a good night's rest did wonders for Ralph, who appeared back to his old self on Sunday, in time for his flight home. Ralph was one of the last animals to leave. The Bonobo monkeys had flown back to Germany on Friday, the epileptic cat a day earlier. And the rest of the animals were slowly making their way home, too.

After six days it was over. Nobody had asked Bonnie Harris or Linda Humby or Vi Tucker or Doc Tweedie to volunteer their time and energy. They just did it automatically. They didn't give any thought to what it cost—the food, the medical attention, the medication. They considered those animals to be their guests, no different from the human passengers.

When the last flight left Sunday afternoon, Harris went home and, for the first time in a week, watched the news. She had caught bits and pieces of the pictures showing the destruction in the States but hadn't had the time to watch. Nor had she really wanted to. She and the other workers at the SPCA shelter had been pulling double duty all week—caring for the animals at the airport as well as all of the animals in their shelter in town. Now, like Ralph, all she wanted was a good night's sleep.

∎

One hundred and twenty-six hours passed between the time the first plane landed in Gander on Tuesday and the last plane departed on Sunday. It would take several more days for the town to recover physically—the shelters cleaned, the schools reopened, the stores restocked—but much longer for the people to absorb the magnitude of what had happened.

In the past, it had always been easy for the citizens of Gander to drown out events in other parts of the world because they always seemed so far removed. Gander, after all, was a safe place to live. A community that prided itself on unlocked doors and friendly neighbors. Now they'd seen how a tragedy more than a thousand miles away could touch their lives directly. Not only had the world come to town, but so, too, did the world's problems.

During those six days, people spent so much effort caring for the passengers that they didn't spend any time thinking about what had happened in New York and Washington. And so their reactions were delayed. Coupled with the sadness of seeing their new friends leave, the ensuing stress played out in different ways. In the schools, teachers noticed some students reporting trouble sleeping or seeming unusually anxious. Diana Sacrey, a guidance counselor at Gander Collegiate, told them not to worry. It would pass. And eventually it did. What remained was a feeling of satisfaction.

Soon after the last plane left Gander, the provincial government in St. John's contacted town hall and offered to pay for a giant party for all of the volunteers, as a way of thanking them for giving up so much of their time to help the stranded passengers. Town leaders accepted, believing their citizens had earned a pat on the back. And if the provincial government was willing to pay for it, all the better. As word spread, however, people in town overwhelmingly decided it wasn't right.

Given the horrific events in the United States, this was not the time for revelry. More than that, though, there was no reason to throw a party just because they had helped a group of people who were in trouble. What other choice was there? How could you not help someone in trouble?

At that point the mayor did the only thing he could do. He thanked the provincial government for the generous offer, but told them the town had decided to cancel plans for the party. There was no need for a celebration. They did what they did for one reason only—it was the Newfie way.

EPILOGUE

Hannah, Kevin, and Dennis O'Rourke, FDNY Medal Day,
1988.

On September 23, firefighter Kevin O'Rourke's body was
recovered amid the 1.8 million tons of debris that had once
been the World Trade Center. Officials believe O'Rourke was
in a stairwell inside the North Tower, somewhere between the
sixty-fifth and the seventieth floors, when it collapsed. After
he was found, his body was placed onto a stretcher, draped in
an American flag, and carried out by a team of his fellow firefighters, including his captain, Phil Ruvolo.

The next afternoon, when Kevin's remains were positively

identified, a delegation from the fire department drove to his home in Hewlett, Long Island. When Maryann saw the men standing on her front stoop, in their full dress uniforms, she knew in her heart why they were there. "Maryann, we found Kevin," Ruvolo said.

Through tears, she thanked the men for finding her husband. Everyone in the family was still praying for a miracle and that Kevin would be found alive, but after so many days, Maryann had steeled herself for the possibility that he was dead. Privately she feared they would never find his body and that Kevin would not receive a proper funeral Mass and burial.

Patricia O'Keefe, Kevin's sister, was also at the house when the news was delivered. It would fall upon her to tell her parents, Hannah and Dennis. As Ruvolo and the others comforted Maryann, Patricia drove to her parents' home in nearby Cedarhurst. She tried to compose herself on the ride over, but realized that telling her parents Kevin was dead would be the most difficult thing she had ever done in her life. When she walked in the house, her father was in the living room. "They found him, Dad," Patricia said. "He's gone, though. Kevin's gone."

The two held each other and cried. They stopped when they realized they still had to tell Hannah, who was upstairs getting ready to drive over to Maryann's house. As Patricia and Dennis reached the top of the stairs, Hannah was waiting for them in the hallway. She could tell what had happened by their expressions. "Oh no," she cried, "not my Kevin. Not my Kevin." Patricia had never seen her mother, who was always so strong, in so much pain. It startled her. And this anguish is an image she will never forget.

The funeral was held on September 28 at St. Joachim's Church on Long Island. It was one of eight funerals and memorial Masses held for firefighters that day. The mayor of New York, Rudolph Giuliani, attended Kevin's funeral, as did hundreds of firefighters. There was even a Canadian Mountie, who came to pay his respects on behalf of the people of Canada. Kevin's captain offered a eulogy, as did his sister and brother. Kevin's older daughter, Corinne, spoke about how her father had always been a hero to her.

Since the funeral, Hannah goes to St. Joachim's every day and quietly cries through morning Mass. She tells her family that as she kneels and prays, she can see Kevin as a young boy receiving his first Holy Communion, and she can see him years later being confirmed. She cries in the church and then she goes home and tries not to cry again during the day.

Through it all, she has not forgotten the kindness of the people in Gander and continues to write and talk to both Beulah Cooper and Tom Mercer. She hopes to return to Gander during the next year with the rest of her family.

▎

Early Saturday morning, a few hours after George Vitale's flight landed in Newark, the New York State trooper was back to work, coordinating dignitary access to the site of the Trade Center collapse. Vitale couldn't bring himself to visit the site, working instead from the governor's offices in midtown Manhattan. By now he realized there was little hope of his friend David DeRubbio being found alive.

Vitale worked sixteen-hour days, and rather than going home, he slept either in the office or at a nearby hotel. Truth be told, he didn't want to go home. He didn't want to be alone. He'd sleep for a few hours and then go for runs through the streets of Manhattan. Eventually, he returned to his apartment in Brooklyn, and his first morning back, he went for his normal run along the bicycle path near the Verrazano-Narrows Bridge. This time, though, instead of seeing the towers in the distance, he saw only the smoke, which was rising from the fires still burning at the Trade Center site.

Once again he felt overwhelmed by emotion. He cut over to the road above the bike path. It was lined with trees, which obscured his view of southern Manhattan and the gaping void of the towers site. He'd always taken great solace in running—it was like therapy for him—and now a part of that daily routine was forever spoiled. He knew he would never be able to run along that path again, even though it was something he loved doing. He was angry and sad and depressed and still feeling guilty that there wasn't more he could be doing.

The tensions at work were constant. One day he would have to bring in inspectors to test the governor's office for signs of anthrax. The next he would arrange to take a vanload of state senators to Ground Zero so they could see the devastation for themselves. And on another day he'd be working with distraught family members of victims who needed help getting a death certificate for their lost loved one.

Several weeks after he left Gander, Vitale felt himself coming apart. He was sitting at his desk, talking on the phone and dealing with yet another bureacratic problem, when he received a call on his other line. Normally, he never places a person on hold. He just allows the second call to go to his voice mail. Something about this call was different, however. When he answered the second line, he heard a familiar voice. It was Derm Flynn, the mayor of Appleton, Newfoundland. Flynn and Vitale had become friends during the trooper's stay in Appleton. "Just thinking about you, buddy," Flynn said. "How's she going?"

Flynn's voice brought back all the good memories Vitale had about the people in Newfoundland. Their kindness, their strength, their support. He could feel his hands shaking. They spoke for several minutes. Flynn talked about his wife and how everyone in town missed having the passengers around. Flynn asked how everything was going in New York, and Vitale told him. By the time they finished, Vitale felt better than he had felt in weeks. Over the next few months Flynn seemed to call him at just those moments when he was feeling his lowest.

In February, Vitale and another passenger from his flight, Tom McKeon, returned to Newfoundland, where they were the guests of honor at Appleton's annual Winterfest, an event that includes snowmobile races, ax-throwing contests, and a musical production featuring local singers. Vitale plans on going back again in the near future.

A memorial Mass was held for firefighter David DeRubbio on November 10, 2001 at St. Agatha's Roman Catholic Church in Brooklyn. His body was never recovered.

▌

In the weeks following the diverted flights, several towns in Newfoundland held local elections. Gander Mayor Claude Elliott easily won. And in Glenwood, not only was Janet Shaw—the woman who'd scolded Bill Fitzpatrick for staying out late when his mother was worrying about him—reelected to the town council, but because of her tell-it-like-it-is style, she received more votes than any other council member, which promoted her to the position of mayor.

▌

Through the fall of 2001, Texan Deborah Farrar and Marine lieutenant Greg Curtis talked by phone and exchanged notes. They had hoped to get together before the end of the year and see if their budding romance would pick up where it left off in Gambo, but in December, Curtis was sent to Afghanistan. The events of September 11 had brought the two of them together.

And for the time being, the subsequent war on terrorism was going to keep them apart.

When the Afghan capital city of Kabul was captured from the Taliban, Curtis was part of the force assigned to protect the newly reopened U.S. embassy. Farrar and Curtis traded e-mails while he was in Kabul, and Farrar sent him care packages. In one, she packed magazines and food and other items she knew he would like. She also added something special. A little inside joke from their time together. She threw in a pack of bikini underwear—the kind Curtis jokingly told her he had bought at Wal-Mart.

In April, George and Edna Neal flew down to Houston to visit their former houseguests—Farrar, Winnie House, Lana Etherington, and Bill Cash. The Houston tribe feted the Neals, taking them on trips around Texas, hosting parties for them, and generally trying to show them as enjoyable a time as they themselves had had in Gambo. They all remain close friends, and in May 2002, Farrar even flew to England to attend House's wedding.

▌

Cleaning up after the passengers had left, a teacher at Lakewood Academy in Glenwood discovered something amazing on the blackboard of the sixth-grade classroom. Using various colored chalks and crayons, someone had drawn a picture depicting a human body in flight. It was at least three feet by four feet and at the bottom of the blackboard it was signed, MANY THANKS, CLEMENS.

Clemens was a passenger, Clemens Briels, and when teachers at the school did a little further checking, they learned that he was a renowned Dutch artist. In fact, Briels was one of the official artists for the 2002 Winter Olympics in Salt Lake City. The drawing he crafted on the school blackboard was a version of his piece *A Jump for Joy*, one of the paintings he created especially for the Olympic Games and which was on display in Salt Lake City. The principal had the blackboard removed from the wall, framed, and covered with Plexiglas. It now hangs in the school's library.

▌

Before leaving Gander, the Tent Girls, Lisa Zale and Sara Wood, donated all of their equipment to the Knights of Columbus and spent part of the day scrubbing all of the bathrooms in the hall. They just wanted to do something tangible as a way of thanking their hosts. Zale made it home to Dallas in time to take one of her sons to his Little League baseball game, and that night she attended her high school reunion.

Lenny and Maria O'Driscoll spent their last night in Gander gathered around a piano in Doug and Rose Sheppard's home, playing and singing songs. Maria, a classical violinist who toured Europe before moving to the United States, is also well trained on the piano. For the Sheppards, she played a mix of Irish music and a bit of ragtime and then performed a beautiful classical piece by Enrico Toselli: "Toselli's 78." Lenny didn't have the time to look up any of his old relatives in Newfoundland, but his time in Gander rekindled his love for his native land and he promised to return soon.

Lufthansa Captain Reinhard Knoth asked his passengers if they wanted to continue on to New York or return to Frankfurt. Not surprisingly, the Americans on the plane wanted to go on to the states and the Europeans wanted to turn around.

Knoth, however, was starting to feel the same way about this journey as his passenger, Werner Baldessarini, the Hugo Boss chairman. In Knoth's mind this was such a unique event, such a special moment in time, he believed the passengers and the crew should see it through together. On Saturday, Lufthansa

Flight 400 was given clearance to proceed on to New York and Knoth had made special arrangements with the airline. When the flight landed Saturday afternoon at JFK, the American passengers were free to leave, while the European passengers walked off the plane, across the terminal, and immediately onto a waiting Lufthansa plane that would take them directly to Frankfurt. For his part, Baldessarini wasn't bothered by having to first fly to New York. Touching down in the city and then flying home to Germany, gave him time to reflect, and symbolically at least, it helped close the circle of events from the last week.

After the last plane left Gander, wild rumors circulated around town about who had actually stayed there. Several people would swear that former vice president Al Gore was on a private plane that landed up the road in Stephenville, where he was secretly whisked aboard an American military jet and flown to the United States. Another rumor had Gore being led under heavy security onto a ferry in the town of Port aux Basques.

As it turned out, Gore had spent September 11 in Europe, not in Newfoundland. And he flew home several days after the tragedy. He never stopped in Newfoundland.

Another urban legend: fashion guru Calvin Klein was in Gander. The rumor had him sleeping inside the auditorium for the College of the North Atlantic at night and wandering the town by day. He reportedly didn't want anyone to know who he was, so he always wore a hat and sunglasses.

One rumor that did turn out to be true: the wife and children of actor Woody Harrelson were stranded in Gander on their way home from a vacation in Europe. The star of *The People vs. Larry Flynt*, *Natural Born Killers*, and *Kingpin* wasn't with his family, but was able to talk to them by phone. The Harrelson family spent their time quietly in Gander and then went home with everyone else when their flight was cleared to leave.

One Hollywood personality who was in Gander was actress Marisa Berenson, one of the world's first supermodels, who'd made her screen debut in *Death in Venice* in 1970 and won critical acclaim for her role in 1972's *Cabaret,* in which she played Natalie Landauer, the Jewish department-store heiress who is given English lessons by Liza Minnelli's character and then comes to her later for sexual advice. In 1975, she starred as Ryan O'Neal's wife in *Barry Lyndon,* the Stanley Kubrick visual masterpiece set in eighteenth-century Ireland.

Less than a month before her plane was diverted to Gander, a story about Berenson and her sister, Berry, was featured in *The New York Times Sunday Magazine.* The magazine noted that Yves Saint Laurent had dubbed Marisa "the girl of the seventies," and *Elle* magazine crowned her "the most beautiful girl in the world." In recent years she had continued to act, appearing recently in a play on Broadway.

By a cruel coincidence, while Marisa was flying from Paris to New York on September 11, her sister was on one of the planes taken over by the hijackers. Berry Berenson, a well-known photographer and the widow of actor Anthony Perkins, was aboard American Airlines Flight 11, en route from Boston to Los Angeles, when it crashed into the North Tower of the Trade Center.

The two sisters had been extremely close since their childhood. Their grandmother was Elsa Schiaparelli, the famed couturiere whose use of shocking pink electrified the fashion world. Their great-uncle was the art historian Bernard Berenson. As children, they were taught to dance by Gene Kelly and developed a sense of style under the tutelage of Diana Vreeland, the legendary editor in chief of *Vogue* magazine. As adults, they were part of the international jet set, had been regulars at Studio 54, and counted Andy Warhol and Diane von Furstenberg as their friends.

"I'm not complaining," Marisa had told the *Times*, "but everyone has their pain and tragedies in life—it doesn't matter how famous or blessed you are."

Six weeks after leaving Lewisporte, Rockefeller Foundation vice-president Denise Gray-Felder still hadn't heard from either Lewisporte Middle School principal Pam Coish about their offer to furnish the school with new computers or from Pastor Russell Bartlett about a grant to the church. Neither of them, it turned out, wanted to seem pushy. By not calling, they were giving the foundation a chance to reconsider their pledge.

Gray-Felder asked if Coish had made a decision about the computers. Did the school need something else? Coish said the computers would be a wonderful gift. Initially the school had asked for less than $35,000 to replace the thirty-five computers. Gray-Felder realized school officials didn't want to appear greedy or to be taking advantage of the foundation. She summarily rejected the number as being too low. She wanted to make sure the kids had top-of-the-line computers. The school finally agreed to accept a total grant of $52,500, which came to $1,500 a computer.

Pastor Bartlett was equally circumspect. After hemming and hawing, he finally agreed to accept a grant of $15,000, which went into a fund to help people in need.

The people from the Rockefeller Foundation weren't the only ones who offered donations to their hosts. In nearly all of the shelters, passengers passed the hat, often generating several thousand dollars in cash, which they gave to the group or school that had taken them in. One passenger pledged to replace the roof on one of the local churches, while others wrote checks directly to the Canadian Red Cross, the Salvation Army, or one of the town governments, as a sign of appreciation.

The most ambitious fund-raising effort was taken up by the passengers of Delta Flight 15, who stayed in the town of Lewisporte. While they were flying to Atlanta from Newfoundland, a small group of passengers talked about how they wished there was something they could do to thank everyone. They realized Newfoundland was going through tough economic times, and towns such as Lewisporte had been particularly hard hit.

One of the passengers, a Dr. Robert Ferguson from North Carolina, had the idea of creating a college scholarship fund, which could select a deserving student every year. Others thought it was a great idea, and before long another passenger, Shirley Brooks, convinced the flight crew to let her get on the plane's public-address system to announce the idea to the 217 other people on board. Pledge sheets were quickly passed around. And by the time the plane reached Atlanta, more than $15,000 was pledged for the fund. Today, the group has its own Web site—www.deltaflight15.org—and the money collected is being overseen by a well-respected charitable foundation in the United States. The fund, known officially as the Gander Flight 15 Scholarship Fund, was preparing to announce its first scholarship recipient in Lewisporte as this book was going to press in during the summer of 2002.

▐

For Clark and Roxanne Loper and their adopted daughter Alexandria, the final leg of the long journey home was not without problems. After they had stopped in Tennessee on Monday night, Roxanne's flu had progressed to the point where she was having trouble breathing. A pediatric nurse by profession, she knew she needed to see a doctor. Early Tuesday morning she went to the emergency room of the local hospital, where doctors told her what she already feared—her flu had turned into pneumonia.

Roxanne didn't want to stop. They were so close to their home in Alto, Texas. She just wanted to get there and have this entire trip be over. She missed her house with the brown tin roof. She missed her ranch with the horses and the chickens and the dogs. She missed seeing her parents. She missed being alone with her husband and sleeping in her own bed. And most of all she missed holding her other daughter, Samantha, whom they had adopted a year earlier.

Rather than admit Roxanne into the hospital, the doctors filled her full of antibiotics and let her go. On Wednesday, the Lopers crossed into Texas. Their first stop was Clark's parents' house in Tyler. A banner welcoming them back greeted them when they arrived. Roxanne's mother pulled up thirty minutes later with Samantha. The two-year-old had grown so much since they had left that Roxanne started to cry. Although both sets of parents were anxious to hear about their adventure, Roxanne wanted to leave. There would be plenty of time to catch up later. Since picking up Alexandria in Kazakhstan, they had traveled nearly 8,000 miles by plane, ferry, and automobile, and now the only thing that separated them from their home was a fifty-two-mile drive down U.S. Highway 69 from Tyler to Alto. They raced down that last patch of roadway, and with each passing mile marker, Roxanne's spirits lifted. They pulled into the driveway and, like kids running down the stairs on Christmas morning, couldn't wait to get through the door. It was quiet and peaceful, and they were all together, safe and sound, a new family, a complete family. Walking through the entrance, Roxanne said the only thing that made sense in that moment, two words she'd waited more than a week to say: "We're home."